D0906985

LANCASTER COUNTY

The Red Rose of Pennsylvania

LANCASTER COUNTY

The Red Rose of Pennsylvania

JOHN WARD WILLSON LOOSE
"Partners in Progress" by Gary G. Martin and Donald L. Collins
CCA Publications, Inc.

Contents

SASQUESAHANOK

A Diversity of People

The Susquehannock Fort built by the Iroquois along the Susquehanna River was central to a dispute between William Penn and Lord Baltimore over the boundary between Pennsylvania and Maryland. Early 20th-century research revealed Baltimore's claim was valid. The fort was on the 40th degree of latitude, further north than Penn had assumed.

Among the American colonies no province was more pluralistic or cosmopolitan than Pennsylvania, and nowhere in Penn's Woods did this diversity flourish with more richness and vigor than in what was to become Lancaster County. Late-19th-century historians attributed the genius of Lancaster Countians to the ethnic characteristics supposedly possessed by its natives. A more acceptable explanation for the thought and behavior patterns—the culture—of Lancastrians is suggested by their responses historically to challenges, primarily those presented by their environment.

The relationship that developed between man and nature, as each confronted the other, produced complex and unique situations. Out of this constant process of action and reaction, resistance and acquiescence, challenge and response, has evolved a principled pragmatism. Whether the challenges were religious, economic, or environmental in origin, the work ethic was ingrained deeply in the typical Lancastrian.

Prehistoric Lancaster County was inhabited by the ancestors of Native Americans nearly 11 centuries ago. During the Late Woodland culture, "Shenks Ferry people" established their villages along the Susquehanna River in Manor and Conestoga townships; they were here from approximately A.D. 1150 to A.D. 1550. Susquehannock Indians built their communities along the Susquehanna River and on streams inland from the river from approximately A.D. 1575 to A.D. 1675. Other tribes of Native Americans—the Nanticokes, the Conoys or Piscataways, the Tuscaroras, and displaced Delawares—stayed in Lancaster County for varying lengths of time as they sought fertile soil and abundant game and fish.

The last Native Americans in the area were the Conestoga Indians who were former captives of Susquehannock tribes and remnants of Seneca tribes. Conestoga Indiantown in Manor Township was home to approximately 20 inhabitants in 1763 when revenge-seeking Scots from the Paxtang area massacred the entire community.

By the time European settlers began establishing communities in Lancaster County the local Native American population was relatively small and consisted largely of Conestoga Indians who eked out a living growing produce and making baskets they peddled to the settlers. More aggressive and occasionally hostile Indians resisted those settlers who ventured into the further reaches of Lancaster County. Competition for land, game, fishing, and

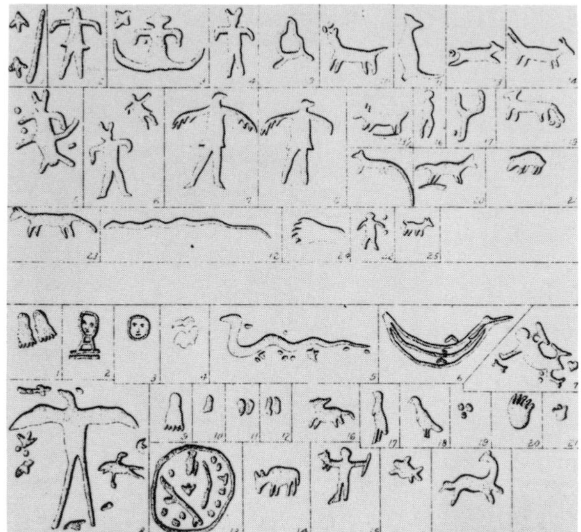

American Indians first came to Pennsylvania about 15,000 years ago, long before the Susquehannocks and Conestogas who lived in the area when white men arrived. Many islands and the shoreline along the Susquehanna River contained petroglyphs that were moved to the state museum and to North Museum in Lancaster. Casts were made of the larger rocks before hydroelectric power plants were built on the river.

fur-bearing animals created bad feelings between the Indians and settlers on the frontier. Occasionally violence and even murder occurred. Relations between the Native Americans and more concentrated communities of white settlers in Lancaster County tended to be harmonious. When violence occurred, the cause usually was drunkenness.

Lack of economic opportunities and rigid land-tenure systems forced most Pennsylvania settlers to break their ties with Europe. Religious wars had laid waste vast areas of the Rhineland, causing severe economic problems for several generations. Although by the early 1700s religious persecution was more a memory than a reality, the threat occasionally sparked the decision to come to Pennsylvania. William Penn's land of promise seemed a beacon of hope to those who realized too well the warfare and destruction of the human spirit caused by state-sponsored religion—and also beckoned to ambitious immigrants.

Before Lancaster County was erected on May 10, 1729 (the English "erected" counties), Pennsylvania consisted of three original counties—Bucks, Philadelphia, and Chester—all created in 1682 by William Penn, the Quaker proprietor. Chester County was defined vaguely as that area from Philadelphia County as far west as the South Mountain and as far north as the Blue Mountain.

As settlers moved into the wild backwoods of Chester County, problems of law enforcement developed. Clearly, local government was needed. In 1718 Chester County created Conestoga Township, which included all the area west and north of the Octoraro Creek. Often without bothering to acquire rights from the proprietor, Scots from Ulster took up land in the Chikiswalungo Valley near the Susquehanna River. They hadn't relished their transplanting from Scotland to Ulster at the hands of the English, nor did they find their Irish neighbors agreeable. Once in Philadelphia, they tarried no longer than necessary and moved westward.

Germans rapidly filled up the broad, flat limestone valley of the Conestoga River. Chester County created another new township, West Conestoga, in 1720; it included land north of the Pequea Creek. That move brought the wrath of the Scots upon the heads of the English government, for Conestoga was an Indian name and Scots regarded Indians as natural enemies. The Quaker administration, always unhappy with the belligerent Scots, yielded in 1722, and West Conestoga was changed to Donegal Township. Meanwhile the influx of

William Penn was 32 years old when he received his charter from King Charles II, who was indebted to Penn's father, a British admiral. The religious toleration encouraged by Penn attracted large numbers of Europeans to settle in Penn's Woods, or Pennsylvania.

St. John's Episcopal Church of Pequea (Compassville) is on the boundary of Lancaster and Chester counties. This communion set (flagon, plate, and chalice) was made in 1766, and is of the style produced by famed Lancaster pewterer Johann Christopher Heyne. Lancaster silversmiths and pewterers were highly skilled craftsmen considered among the finest of the colonies.

settlers, many of them Welsh, to the headwaters of the Pequea Creek caused the formation of Pequea Township in 1721. No specific boundaries were recorded for this township, but it was included in the present Salisbury and East Earl townships. A township named West Strasburg was never officially established nor even placed before the court, but nevertheless was cited in early deeds. It probably included parts of today's East Lampeter, West Lampeter, and Lancaster townships, and even part of Lancaster city.

Lands west and north of present Lancaster County were unorganized and possessed no local government until the Lancaster County Quarter Sessions Court approved the creation of townships between 1729 and 1785 in what later became York, Cumberland, Dauphin, Northumberland, Lebanon, and Berks counties.

Indian traders traveled through the Susquehanna Valley from the earliest days of the colony. Here and there they maintained trading posts, often connected to each other and the coastal market town by trails that eventually became roads. Peter Bezaillion's trading post on the Susquehanna River in Donegal Township was connected to his home base at Compassville by a trail that bore his name: Old Peter's Road. That road later formed the northern boundaries of East Hempfield, Manheim, and Leacock townships.

Lancaster County's first permanent settlers, tradition claims, were the Swiss Mennonites that took up residence between Lampeter and Willow Street. The Herrs, Mylins, and Kendigs were noteworthy members of that small band of pioneers. More recent research provides two rivals to the claim of first settlers. A Scot named Gault was established in Salisbury Township by 1710, and an English Quaker family was keeping the hearth fire burning in Little Britain Township possibly prior to 1710. The Herr-Mylin-Kendig community made a great and permanent mark upon the county's heritage. Germanic Switzerland and the German Rhineland were quite similar culturally. Not always is it possible to say with certainty that one family came from Switzerland and another from Germany.

French Huguenots (Protestants) began arriving in 1712 and generally settled in the area near present-day Paradise and Strasburg. Their names, occasionally Anglicized, betray their Gallic origins. Madame Marie Ferree led the little community, and thereby became Lancaster County's first "outstanding woman" in a heritage that now numbers many hundreds of acknowledged women in the arts, sciences, government, medicine, and commerce. Early records mention the family names of LeFevre, Diller, Mathiot, DuBois, and Bushong (Anglicized from Beauchamps). In religion the Huguenots of Lancaster mainly affiliated with the Reformed, Lutheran, and Presbyterian churches.

Following on the heels of the Huguenots were the Scottish Presbyterians who settled in what was to become Donegal Township. A Presbyterian church was built at Donegal Springs; it served not only

Donegal Springs Presbyterian Church was built in 1721 to serve the Scottish Presbyterians who had emigrated from Ulster, Ireland, in the early 1700s. During the American Revolution, a messenger supposedly brought news of British soldiers invading Chester County, whereupon the able-bodied men of the congregation gathered around the oak tree in front of the church, swore allegiance to the patriotic cause, then marched off to participate in the Battle of Brandywine. Located near Maytown in East Donegal Township, this church continues to serve an active congregation. The majestic oak succumbed to old age and was taken down in 1991.

as the focal point of the community of Scots but it gave birth to one of the nation's most historic presbyteries. A second wave of Scots was diverted to the Drumore area near the Maryland border by the Quaker government, it is thought, because the Quakers could not repel the Marylanders without using force, an activity unthinkable to the more devout Friends. Presbyterian churches sprang up at Chestnut Level, Muddy Run, Middle Octoraro, and Little Britain.

Local tradition has maintained the Scots were indifferent farmers and lacked the patience of the Germans in building fertile farmland. Recent research suggests the Scots compared favorably with the Germans when they put down their roots and overcame their wanderlust. It is true, of course, that many Scots continued moving westward and their places were taken by German farmers.

English Quakers and members of the Church of England (Anglicans) began arriving about 1716 and settled in a belt running east to west across the girth of the county, from Salisbury to Hempfield townships.

Development of the county seat drew Englishmen to that "urban" center but never in numbers that would rival the Germans. Welsh settlers, mostly members of the Church of England, occupied the eastern areas of the county, providing such place names as Caernarvon and Brecknock townships, and Bangor.

During the 1720s the central limestone plain of the county became home to hundreds of German farmers and mechanics representing every mode of religious expression, from the highly liturgical Lutherans and cerebral Calvinists (German Reformed) to the extremely individualistic sects, including the Anabaptists, which fell into two major groups: Mennonites and German Baptist Brethren (Dunkers). Among the Mennonites were the Amish that migrated slowly down the Conestoga Valley in the latter half of the 18th century and many splinter groups led by charismatic ideologists. Not all Germans found the impersonality of the Lutheran and Reformed churches satisfying to their spiritual needs. Later in the 18th century these disaffected persons flocked to the "German Methodist" congregations: United

Salisbury Monthly (Quaker) Meeting was established in Sadsbury Township in 1723. The present stone meetinghouse was built in 1747 and is regarded as the shrine of Lancaster County's Religious Society of Friends.

Brethren in Christ and the Evangelical Association.

The German Baptist Brethren experienced defections. The most colorful was that of Johann Conrad Beissel, founder of the Ephrata Cloister. Beissel observed Saturday, the seventh day of the week, as the Sabbath and his movement resulted in the German Seventh-Day Baptist Society, which eventually took over his defunct community. A small and quite conservative religious association known as the River Brethren was formed in western Lancaster County as a theological compromise between the German Baptists and the Mennonites. Still active today, in appearance and custom they resemble somewhat the Old Order Mennonites. The men wear broad-brimmed hats not unlike the Amishmen. Like the Horning Mennonites, they cover the chromium parts of their motorcars with black paint.

During colonial days Lancaster's ethnic and religious diversity fostered a tolerance and harmony forged out of necessity, making a united effort against the relentless frontier. All energies—none could be wasted on bickering or foolish contentiousness—had to be turned to survival in the wilderness. Such diversity produced a wealth of worship patterns and liturgies; it generated within churches a continuum of expression ranging from the liberal to the conservative; from the plain and austere to the rich pageantry of old established churches. Lancaster County also was the scene of many schisms—perhaps more than found in any other part of the nation—as ideas and institutions clashed toward the end of its first century of growth. Lancastrians seemed to prefer forming new congregations rather than fighting long and acrimonious battles within their churches.

Lancaster County often is considered to be an exceptionally conservative community. But the county always has been balanced by a strong and influential liberal tradition, which reflects the individualistic spirit manifested by the Republic's founding fathers—great faith in the ability of free men and women to manage their own lives and enterprises with a minimum of regulation by the government, however benign. From its Quakers, Moravians, Swedenborgians, German university-trained clergy, and German sectarians has come a subtle, albeit efficacious, spirit that cuts through orthodoxy and blunts the hard edges of political and religious

Every town seems to have its characters, and Lancaster is no exception. One such local eccentric was Hiram Kroom, a Scottish scissors grinder who possessed a powerful voice, which he used to good advantage in St. James' choir.

Wilhelm Rheafuss' Union Hotel, opposite the Pennsylvania Railroad depot on East Chestnut Street, was doubtless a welcomed rest stop for weary German immigrants in 1870s Lancaster County.

Contemporary Mennonite women maintain the old ways in the midst of modern Lancaster. (Mark E. Gibson)

conservatism. Extreme or obviously impractical solutions to problems meet with little acceptance among Lancastrians.

Scottish influence can be detected in Lancaster speech, particularly in the clearly enunciated r, although northeastern county "Dutchmen" mute the r sound similar to the New York-spoken r. Another vestige of the Scottish presence is the expression "redding up," meaning to tidy up a disorderly area. To this day some Quaker families in southern Lancaster County employ thee and thou in addressing members of their families; it is a token of closeness and respect for human dignity.

Many Amish persons are trilingual, using German in their lengthy worship services, Pennsylvania-German dialect in conversation among themselves and other countrymen, and English (usually superior to that spoken by the general population) when talking with worldly folk. Visitors to Lancaster County frequently ask if the Amish are a major influence in the culture and life of the Red Rose County. But, influence of the Amish cannot be measured statistically. Certainly in recent decades tourism has had a major effect in Lancaster County; it brings millions of visitors to the county and the Amish are the principal attraction despite the presence of many historic buildings and museums not related to Amish life.

Most of the nearly 20,000 Amish in Lancaster County are Old Order Amish. They are the least progressive of the Amish; they maintain the old ways and are most resistant to the worldly life around them. They worship in their houses rather than in church buildings. Carriages and wagons drawn by horses are their mode of transportation although the adult Amish may ride in but not own motor cars. Electricity purchased from a power company is prohibited. Power supplied by gasoline and diesel engines is acceptable. Wind power, water power, and compressed air often are used to operate pumps and other machinery. Telephone use is discouraged because that convenience is conducive to idle talk and gossip. Horses and mules are used to draw farm machinery. Tractors, rubber-tired machines, and wagons are prohibited. Indoor plumbing is permissible if electrical power is not used to pump water.

Despite the apparent austere life-style of the Amish, they are a very pleasant, delightful people. They work hard but enjoy life. They have large families and the children are educated in Amish schools until they complete the eighth grade. Although the curriculum is basic and the teachers are not educated beyond the eighth grade, the children acquire a knowledge of reading, writing, arithmetic, history, and geography that would put many first-rate public schools to shame. Moreover, hard work, honesty, and courtesy are essential parts of the curriculum. Amish youth, like the teenagers of more worldly society, have been known to have drinking parties, drive fast cars, and do other mischief. As soon as they are ready to become members of the church, all the worldly behavior must end. The penalty may be severe. Shunning, while not imposed frequently, cuts off the punished from all communication and association with other Amish, including their family.

The life-style of the Amish is not derived from a strange theology but from a desire to be "not of this world." Their religious beliefs are based on the Mennonite version of Protestantism. A smaller group of Amish that have adopted some worldly ways are called Conservative Amish Mennonites. Other minor groups of Amish prefer a more evangelistic mode of worship.

The time line between the Pennsylvania-German and the German immigration is marked at 1808. Many persons from the Rhineland and other parts of what was to become the German Empire continued to settle in Lancaster County. During the 19th century large numbers of Germans from Bavaria, Baden, Wurttemberg, and Saxony made Lancaster city and Columbia their homes. Unlike the earlier immigration, Roman Catholics were numerous among those who found homes and jobs here. In Lancaster and Columbia entire German parishes were established. Like the earlier immigrants these later arrivals were deeply religious persons with a strong work ethic. Lutheran and German Reformed churches also gained membership from 19th-century immigration.

The potato famine and other economic deprivations in Ireland caused immigration to America in the early and middle 19th century. Lancaster County, along with much of Pennsylvania, was caught up in the building of internal improvements—roads, canals, and railroads. Irish labor and Irish contractors were used extensively in these major projects. Approximately a half-dozen Irish contractors in Lancaster became quite prosperous and found themselves busy in the civic life of the community. Their philanthropic spirit manifested itself widely in church and community.

Lancaster County had the fourth largest number of African slaves among Pennsylvania counties in 1790. Many of the African-Americans were employed around the iron works and other enterprises of the British settlers. In Lancaster borough the usual role for African-Americans was that of house servants for well-to-do merchants, innkeepers, and members of the professions. Members of the black community to an unusually high degree were "free" and in the 18th and 19th centuries were property owners, members of a rising middle class. Stephen Smith and William Whipper of Columbia were outstanding businessmen. Numerous African-Americans operated their own businesses. Black leaders encouraged the growth of churches and schools in Lancaster, Columbia, Marietta, and other parts of Lancaster County. Bethel African Methodist Episcopal Church in Lancaster dates from 1817, and the earliest congregation for persons of color was established in Columbia early in the 1820s. Similar congregations appeared during the 19th century in Marietta, Fulton Township, and the Welsh Mountain.

Not all members of the black community enjoyed middle-class status. As with the underclass of all human societies, there were neighborhoods notorious for crime and problems associated with poverty and alcoholism.

Toward the end of the 19th century emigrants from Russia and Poland found Lancaster a thriving

Honoring the sacrifice of a war that ended British interference in American affairs, members of the Robert Fulton Chapter of the U.S. Daughters of 1812 mark the gravesite of local soldiers.

A 1900-era character in downtown Lancaster was banjo-playing Jake Parks, who earned a living gathering old newspapers and rags. He died in 1928, at the age of 92.

Lancaster's curb markets were an old institution that existed along the downtown streets until 1927, when they were abolished by law. In this 1926 scene along South Duke Street just south of East King Street, several Amish women tend a stand along with their more worldly neighbors. The demise of curb markets promoted greater activity in the market houses and created roadside stands outside the city.

market for consumer goods. The more successful country peddlers opened stores, some of which remain in the same families generations later. The famed Seligman Brothers, stockbrokers of New York, had their beginnings as peddlers in Lancaster. Congregation Chizuk Emunah dates from 1887, and Congregation Hagudah Sholom separated from the earlier Orthodox group in 1892. Congregation Degal Israel was chartered in 1896 and the Kesher Torah synagogue, started in 1922, merged back into Degel Israel in 1920, joining all Orthodox groups that had original separate existences. Temple Shaarai Shomayim, the original Jewish congregation of 1856, represented Reform Judaism.

At the very end of the 19th century immigrants from Italy and southern Europe gradually settled in Lancaster where they became part of the solidly established tradition of law-abiding, industrious citizenry. Early in the 20th century immigrants from Greece—principally the island of Cos—fitted into the social fabric of Lancaster to add materially to the Lancaster tradition. Other immigrants in small numbers and groups from Armenia and other Middle Eastern nations found homes and jobs here.

Early in the 1950s American citizens from Puerto Rico were brought to Lancaster as migrant farm and cannery workers. They soon discovered Lancaster County offered many economic opportunities, and their relatives and friends joined them. Latinos and other people from the Caribbean islands joined them in Lancaster's labor market. According to the 1990 census the Hispanic population of Lancaster city was approximately 11,500 people although a more accurate count probably would be closer to 15,000. Approximately one person in four in Lancaster is Hispanic. The Hispanic population presents a picture of great contrasts. A small but enterprising middle class has emerged to take its part in the social, political, and economic life of Lancaster. It has established churches and other organizations to assist less fortunate, less well-educated, members of the Hispanic community whose inability to use the English language has been a serious drawback in finding well-paying jobs.

The Spanish American Civic Association (SACA) is one of the organizations that has been helping to solve housing, health, job, and domestic problems. Among its responsibilities are feeding the elderly, furnishing day care, job training, counseling, youth programs, adult education, parenting skills, and operating the North Ann Street School of Business and Trade. The association operates a Spanish language radio station. Carlos Graupera, Executive Director since 1973, takes pride in the many accomplishments of SACA, but recognizes the need for greater community involvement. With each passing year, more Hispanic merchants, business persons, and skilled clerical workers enter the economic life of Lancaster. Much of the Hispanic population lives in the area between South Water Street and East King Street.

Following the war in Vietnam, refugees from Southeast Asia, often sponsored by local churches, arrived in Lancaster County, completing the multi-ethnic social fabric established thousands of years ago by the Native Americans, themselves descendants of Asians. With a great appreciation for the advantages of education, many of the southeast Asian residents have excelled academically in local schools and colleges. Lancaster Countians brought up on diets of meat and potatoes, sauerkraut and chicken pot pie, now find numerous Oriental restaurants around Lancaster offering a vast variety of exotic foods to add flavor to the cultural richness of Lancaster County diversity.

Natural Endowments

Lancaster County is 941 square miles or more than 602,000 acres in size. The county is in the Piedmont Province and can be divided into the Triassic Lowlands, the Conestoga Plain, and the Southeastern Uplands. The Triassic Lowlands arch across northern Lancaster County with the Furnace Hills at the crest. These rocks were formed about 230 to 215 million years ago. Occupying the large central part of the county is the highly fertile, limestone Conestoga Plain. Geologists place the age of the plain at approximately 600 to 300 million years. Somewhat older are the Piedmont Uplands in the southern third of the county. The more erosion-resistant rock of the Triassic Lowlands and portions of the Piedmont Uplands account for the hills and narrow valleys. Softer limestone formations have produced the soil that has enabled Lancaster County farmers, beginning with Native Americans, to create the famed "Garden Spot of America."

Scattered throughout the county are numerous deposits of iron, silver, lead, zinc, nickel, and chrome ores. Lime used for soil dressing and masonry construction was produced in great quantities from Lancaster County quarries and kilns during the 19th century. Greenish serpentine rock underlies portions of southern Lancaster County. Cocalico sandstone, a conglomerate, formerly was used in making millstones for grist mills. Presence of slate in the southwestern part of the county gave rise to a prosperous slate industry during the past century. Various schists and shales are found.

Generations of Lancastrians gratified their "sweet tooth" at G. W. Gibbs Confectionery at 339 West Orange Street. Gibbs' ice cream was said to be the best in Lancaster. This picture made in the 1910 era caught part of the George Gibbs family.

HFSchopf

C H A P T E R T W O

The County in Penn's Woods

Lancaster County's first court was held at John Postlethwaite's tavern on Long Lane in Conestoga Township on August 5, 1729. John Wright, who had the honor of naming Lancaster County, presided. The ancient log building, later enlarged and covered with clapboard, still survives.

When Lancaster County was established, the provincial government reminded the new commissioners some important tasks had to be accomplished. A county seat had to be selected, and a courthouse and jail erected. In 1729 Lancaster County's most influential citizens were clustered about a hamlet known as Wright's Ferry on the Susquehanna River. John Wright, Robert Barber, and Samuel Blunston were the movers and shakers; they also were Quakers, which the Philadelphians found most agreeable. Barber, the first sheriff, built a log jail at Wright's Ferry, hoping that would make the river community the place for the county seat. But several miles southeast of Wright's Ferry, along the Old Conestoga Road near Rock Hill, John Postlethwaite kept an inn, and he was able to keep up with the news of the day and exert influence on his guests. He also entertained notions of having the county seat at his site, a logical choice since the first county court was held at his inn.

Residents in the eastern part of the county wanted to have the seat of government closer to the center of population, which appealed to the provincial government. Commissioners recommended a tract of some five hundred acres about one mile north of the Conestoga River. The governor, however, wondered who owned the tract and the Provincial Prothonotary Andrew Hamilton, Esquire, checked the records. The tract had been warranted by the proprietor to a Richard Wooller of London. He never took up his rights, leading local officials to assume the tract remained in the hands of the Penns, which technically it did. Wooller had died and his heirs sold the rights to Samuel Arnold of London. Hamilton directed James Steele, then in England buying up old rights for Hamilton, to acquire the tract from Arnold, which he did, paying the princely sum of £30 10s. Steele, the Hamilton agent, took nominal title, which later was granted to Hamilton and Hamilton's son, James.

The socially prominent Andrew Hamilton, often regarded as the most brilliant lawyer in the colonies, intended the Lancaster site to be a good investment for his son and family. The elder Hamilton successfully defended John Zenger in a famous case that established freedom of the press, and he designed Independence Hall.

According to legend, when Hamilton began laying out his town, the principal landmark was an inn kept by George Gibson. It was supposed to be located a hundred yards east of Penn Square on the north side of present East King Street, near a spring and a hickory

Born in this humble stone house in Drumore Township in 1749, Dr. David Ramsay graduated from Princeton and the University of Pennsylvania Medical School. Ramsay moved to South Carolina and was a surgeon during the revolutionary war. He went on to serve in Congress from 1782 to 1786, was President Pro Tempore from 1785 to 1786 and wrote the first history of the American Revolution.

tree. Legend also claims the early settlement was known as Hickory Town.

Hamilton did something thought foolish: he laid out his town a mile away from the Conestoga River, with no good waterway within its limits and isolated from the southern route to Philadelphia by a large swamp. The site was hilly and not conducive to development. Nevertheless, Lancaster Townstead, as it was called, grew and prospered as its inhabitants worked to overcome the hostile environment.

Farms, known then as plantations, already dotted the lands along the Conestoga River and the creeks of Lancaster County by 1730. Hamlets appeared where roads to mills, taverns, and churches intersected. Wright's Ferry (now Columbia) was a thriving village serving travelers to the West as they awaited passage across the Susquehanna River.

As early as 1714 the Great Conestoga Road connected Blue Rock (Washington Borough) to the Delaware River. This crude road crossed the county, passing through the present communities of Christiana, Strasburg, the Hans Herr settlement, Willow Street, Rock Hill, and Blue Rock. Very little of the road remains. Travelers from Philadelphia had to leave the Great Conestoga Road near the Hans Herr settlement, and take a primitive road north on or near the present Eshel-

King's Highway, also known as the Old Philadelphia Pike or Route 340, was laid out around 1733. Numerous inns along the roadway provided accommodations for weary travelers. The Sign of the Bull was an early hostelry in Salisbury Township near Compassville.

man Mill Road to South Duke Street and Rockland Street.

In 1733 the provincial government authorized the construction of the "King's Highway" from Philadelphia to Lancaster, now known as the Old Philadelphia Pike or Route 340. This road was impassable during much of the year. Another major road went from Lancaster to Harris Ferry (now Harrisburg). The Newport Road connected the Grubb furnaces at Mount Hope with Newport in Delaware, passing through present-day Rothsville, Leola, and Gap.

As more settlers arrived and the necessity for getting grain to mills and crops to the market increased, more roads were laid out by authority of the county court. To avoid cutting up farmland, such roads generally followed the angles and boundaries of farms, creating sharp corners annoying to modern motorists.

Not until 1794 when the Philadelphia Lancaster Turnpike was constructed (now Route 30) was Lancaster served by an all-weather road. This turnpike, built by a private company, was constructed on the MacAdam Plan. Large football-size rocks were laid down and packed into place, followed by a layer of softball-size rocks, and last, by a layer of egg-size stones and hard gravel. Rain and melting snow could drain through the rock surface instead of causing deep muddy ruts. Broad-tired Conestoga wagons packed the gravel surface and were charged a low toll. Narrow carriage wheels made ruts in the gravel and were charged more than the heavy wagons.

One spring day in 1736 James Hamilton stood along High Street, the principal thoroughfare of his new town, inhaling the pungent breeze wafting northward from Dark Hazel Swamp and observing the progress of Lancaster town. Houses were rising on the 17 lots purchased the previous year. Ten lots had even been claimed as early as 1730—before Hamilton had a legal right to lay out his town and sell lots. Hamilton may well have acknowledged that having a prominent and politically powerful father steered the project through some legal shoals that would have ruined lesser persons.

Additional streets would be needed. Naming them could demonstrate loyalty to the English monarchy, a not inconsiderable factor in retaining royal favor. The main east-west street, now High Street, became King George Street, while the chief north-south road honored his consort, Queen Caroline. Prince of Wales Street was one block to the west. Orange Street recognized the royal house of King William III. Lancastrians dropped using the full English names long before the American Revolution and those streets became simply King, Queen, Duke, and Prince. Dear to the English heart was the custom of naming streets for trees, nuts, fruits, berries, and vines. James Hamilton was dutybound to surround the royal streets with Chestnut, Lime, Lemon, Mulberry, and Vine streets. Water Street was a pathway along Roaring Brook, a powerful stream bearing an

James Hamilton, son of the celebrated Andrew Hamilton, was Lancaster's founder and proprietor. He was a businessman rather than a politician, and his Whiggish inclinations helped Lancaster become an enterprising community.

From 1763 to 1767, surveyors placed marker stones along the Mason-Dixon line, the boundary between Pennsylvania and Maryland. Five of these stones stood along the line between Lancaster County and Cecil County, Maryland. Dr. Herbert H. Beck (1875–1960), long-time president of the Lancaster County Historical Society, points to the coat-of-arms on the Pennsylvania side of the marker.

Featuring unique half-timbered Germanic architecture, these mid-18th century dwellings on Middle Street (now Howard Avenue) were among the oldest survivors of early Lancaster. Although most of these structures were torn down nearly a century ago, a few of the pre-revolutionary buildings still exist today.

idyllic name that was later transformed into Hoffman's Run before being christened with the final ignominy, Gas House Run.

Hamilton provided his town with one of its first distinctions by locating the county courthouse in the middle of Centre Square, the enlarged intersection of the two principal streets. Lots were provided for a market square at the northwest corner of the center square (now the Central Market and the Heritage Center Museum) and the county prison at the northwest corner of West King and North Prince streets. To encourage sobriety, spirituality, and morality, lots were given for erecting churches.

Upon purchasing a lot, the holder was required to erect within one year a "substantial Dwelling-house of the Dimensions of Sixteen feet square at least, with a good chimney of Brick or Stone, to be laid in or built with Lime or Sand." Hamilton wanted to prevent house fires, of course, but he also specified substantial construction in order to keep out the lower classes unskilled in trades, for he realized the success of his town depended on the development of a population consisting largely of skilled middle-class artisans, merchants, and professionals. In that objective he was extremely successful.

More than 140 lots were developed by 1740, with each year exceeding the previous one in growth. Observers commented on the size of the town and the number of persons and houses, but their estimates vary greatly. Lancaster had about five hundred inhabitants and one hundred houses in 1740. Three independent "towns" adjacent to Hamilton's tract of Lancaster were acquired by 1760. John Musser's "Mussertown" and Dr. Adam Simon Kuhn's "Adamstown" along Church Street and Howard Avenue, and Samuel Bethel's "Bethelstown," in the southwest part along Strawberry and South Prince streets were added to the Hamilton gridiron, giving Lancaster its two diagonal neighborhoods south of Church and Strawberry streets.

By 1742 Lancaster had grown to become one of the largest inland towns in the British Empire. Nearly 750 persons lived in the houses thought to number about 270. Despite the chronic difficulty of collecting rents, the Hamiltons were pleased that their speculative venture was turning out so well. They were so gratified, in fact, that they requested a borough charter for Lancaster in 1742. Reasons given for the request were that great improvements and new buildings were being constructed; that inhabitants were increasing in number; and that there was an urgent necessity for the promotion of trade, industry, rule, and good order.

The charter, granted May 1, 1742 by Governor George Thomas in the name of King George II, contained among other things the condition that "the streets of the said Borough shall forever continue as they are now laid out and regulated." That part of the document was honored with rare scrupulousness, because the borough and later the city, retained its two-mile-square boundaries until the years after World War II.

Thanks to Hamiltonian influence in Philadelphia and London, Lancaster's borough charter was quite liberal. It granted the borough a high degree of autonomy. The borough officials were given great latitude in solving problems that would develop. Self-government in Lancaster was an actuality. Moreover, Lancastrians came to assume gradually their autonomy was a natural state of affairs, a position that would make the townspeople, particularly their leaders, resent the authority of the Provincial Council and the British government in the 1760s. With all the freedom given in the charter, there was one drawback. The borough could not assess property and levy taxes for borough needs.

An event in 1744 propelled Lancaster into the colonial limelight. The town served as the meeting place of the treaty-making sessions of the Six Nations of Indians and the colonies of Maryland, Virginia, and Pennsylvania. Visitors from Maryland and Virginia were astonished at the growth and sophistication of the town in the wilderness.

With the advent of the French and Indian wars of the 1750s Lancaster's artisans and mechanics turned their skills to providing guns, wagons, clothing, and military hardware for the British and colonial militia. Although the struggles occurred on the western frontier of Pennsylvania, no place was as well equipped as Lancaster to supply an army. Soon it became the staging area for the militia, with local residents learning what "quartering troops" involved—an education that evoked unpleasant memories.

From 1730 to 1760 the hamlet of Lancaster evolved into a borough of major economic, political, and social importance in the American colonies. Lancastrians and their community gradually assumed a greater role in history. The town itself, created by a businessman seeking a reasonable return on his investment, attracted a then disproportionate number of skilled mechanics and artisans of the middle class. Enlightened professional men, albeit relatively few in number, encouraged the growth of Whiggery, or the desire for freedom to pursue economic opportunities unhindered by excessive regulation.

Religious needs of the Lancastrians were met by the gradual organization of congregations. The German Reformed and Lutheran congregations were organized at the same time as the town. The Moravian and Roman Catholic churches arrived soon after, followed by the Anglican (Church of England) and Presbyterian.

Geography, too, aided fortuitously the development of Lancaster. The town's location was conducive to the establishment of

George Ross was Lancaster's most illustrious lawyer and wealthiest citizen in the pre-revolutionary era. He was a signer of the Declaration of Independence and active member of the Union Fire Company No. 1.

The country home of George Ross was in the "rural" section of northwest Lancaster City. Ross Street now runs through this tract, and the Ross Street Methodist Church is on the site of this mid-18th-century home.

Saint Mary's Roman Catholic Church at West Vine and South Prince streets was the first Roman Catholic church in Lancaster. The parish dates from the 1730s. The church's first structure, which was constructed in stone and completed in 1761, is pictured in the foreground of this 1875 photograph. Behind it is the second and present church building, which was erected in 1852. This second structure was rebuilt after being damaged in an 1867 fire.

artisan workshops and mercantile business. The distant Conestoga River discouraged the growth of large industries requiring much waterpower in central Lancaster. The availability of skilled artisans and nearby industries and mills, coupled with an experienced mercantile community, thrust Lancaster into the role of manufacturing and supplying goods for winning the French and Indian wars, and for western expansion. Hamilton's town by 1760 had proved itself capable of contributing mightily to the American Revolution that was to follow.

Lancaster's leaders sensed the coming of the Revolution early in the 1770s and committees of Correspondence and Safety were established. When actual fighting began, Lancaster was prepared. Lancaster attorney George Ross, serving in the Continental Congress, signed the Declaration of Independence. William Henry, gunsmith and mechanical inventor, produced weapons, including the remarkable deadly rifles for which Lancaster was famous. Paul Zantzinger's shop turned out uniforms and boots. County furnaces and forges, tanneries, and grist mills produced for the American cause. Dr. Edward Hand left his medical practice to lead troops into battle and become General Hand, confidant of General Washington.

On the home front, Christian Wertz guarded thousands of British and Hessian prisoners of war. Edward Shippen patriotically provided leadership in Lancaster, despite members of his family including Peggy Shippen Arnold, being sympathetic to the English. Mathias Slough, innkeeper, spent most of his time rounding up scarce supplies for the American armies. Attorney Jasper Yeates poured through volumes of law books to determine which laws prevailed in Pennsylvania now that it was independent of the English. Other Lancaster patriots included William Augustus Atlee, Adam Reigart, John Hubley, Alexander Lowery, Casper Schaffner, Charles Hall, and William Bausman.

The British invasion of Philadelphia forced the Continental Congress and the Pennsylvania state government to flee to safer quarters. The state legislature and offices were set up in Lancaster where they remained from September 1777 until the following June. The Continental Congress met in Lancaster on September 27, 1777, thereby making Lancaster the capital of the newly independent United States for a day. Owing to the crowded conditions in Lancaster, the Continental Congress moved to York for nine months. Following the revolutionary war, Lancaster was troubled with a declining economy. Inflation was high and regional competition did not help local businessmen.

Lancastrians became resources in manufacturing by responding abundantly to the challenges of the French and Indian wars, the American Revolution, and the War of 1812, which particularly fostered a strong desire for the young nation to be economically self-sufficient and to be able to manufacture most, if not all, goods used locally. Now Lancaster suffered from a surplus of war-work-generated craft apprentices and much unused craftshop capacity.

The state government once more moved to Lancaster and remained from 1799 to 1812. While this put Lancaster into the political limelight, it did not improve the economy. Between 1808 and 1812 a number of communities vied to secure the state capital seat: Northumberland (Sunbury), Harrisburg, Middletown, Philadelphia, Columbia, and Lancaster. Both Lancaster and Columbia tried to have the United States Congress select one of these towns for the site of the permanent national capital. General Hand had put forth strenuous effort to convince the Congress to pick Lancaster. Wright's Ferry, quickly renamed Columbia to add more weight to its claim, came within one vote of becoming the nation's federal city.

Lancaster and Columbia each desired to become the state capital, with Assemblyman Slaymaker leading the effort to move the state lawmakers and offices back to Lancaster in 1818. Costs and slowness of construction in Harrisburg, lack of good transportation facilities, and remoteness all were cited to persuade the state government to come back to Lancaster. As part of the promotional campaign Lancaster again sought city status, which was granted March 20, 1818 by act of the general assembly. Before the city could celebrate its second birthday, a group of Lancastrians, angered by what they thought were excessive taxes and payroll padding, petitioned the general assembly to repeal the city charter. The effort was unsuccessful. Lancaster, the largest inland community in the United States, was now the third city in Pennsylvania, following Philadelphia (1701) and Pittsburgh (1816).

The city charter created two legislative bodies, a select council consisting of nine members whose qualifications were identical to those required for the state senate, and a common council of 15 members who possessed qualifications for the state house of representatives.

To encourage local industry and agriculture, Lancaster's economic leaders established organizations to generate domestic manufactures and farm production. In 1800 the Lancaster County Society for Promoting of Agriculture, Manufactures, and the Useful Arts was formed. Arguments arose between those who wished to promote manufactures (Hamiltonian Federalists) and the backers of agriculture (Jeffersonian Republicans). The society was headed by F. A. Muhlenberg, and had as its purpose "to procure from the fertile soil of Pennsylvania, every production it is capable of affording; and from the labor and ingenuity of independent citizens every article of manufacture

General Edward Hand, Irish-born physician and military leader, was one of Lancaster's most noted citizens. His close and trusted friendship with General Washington earned him the post of adjutant-general. Hand's fine country home, Rock Ford *has been preserved.*

Lancaster well supplied American troops with munitions during the revolutionary war. In 1778, a powder house stood at the corner of North Duke and James streets.

and the useful arts necessary to render our country happy, prosperous, and truly independent." Farmers and artisans who raised the finest farm products or made the most worthy articles of commerce were to receive premiums including 10-dollar gold medals.

There is no evidence anything came of this effort, but in 1817 the American Society of Lancaster County for the Promotion of

Built in 1795, Lancaster's City Hall was already more than 100 years old by the time this photograph was taken in 1900. Civic leader and merchant M. T. Garvin had the building restored at his own expense in 1923. Today this structure, along with the adjoining 1798 Masonic Hall, is part of the Heritage Center museum complex. The historic Central Market can be seen at the far right.

The White Swan, Lancaster's finest hostelry during the revolutionary period, was located on the southeastern corner of Centre Square during the late 18th and throughout the 19th centuries. This 1850 print shows the inn, now Hubly's Hotel, a few years before its decline and eventual conversion into store buildings.

Domestic Manufactures and National Industry was established by a large number of Lancastrians including every member of the ironmaking fraternity. It, too, has left no evidence of any achievement. Two years later Judge Walter Franklin and John Passmore called a meeting to petition Congress to promote domestic manufactures and the economy. Out of this meeting came the Lancaster County Society for the Encouragement of American Manufactures. The by-laws requested its members purchase only American products.

The local economy continued to suffer. In 1821 the Society for the Promotion of Industry and Prevention of Pauperism was formed. It raised money from its members and used the funds to purchase raw materials that the town's paupers manufactured into textiles and socks. Lancaster's Congressman James Buchanan, then a Federalist, reacted promptly to the Lancaster Friends of American Industry by presenting a vigorous speech in the House of Representatives supporting tariffs to protect domestic industry.

The second decade of the 19th century was a troubled time for land speculators and town developers. Many Lancaster County villages and boroughs began at this time. Others were planned but never developed. It was a time of bankruptcies and sheriff sales involving every class of citizen.

In 1818 the young city was bothered by lack of water. Citizens depended upon wells and the stream that flowed in Water Street. In 1837, prodded by the Union Fire Company No. 1, the city built a water distribution system. Untreated water from the Conestoga River was pumped to a reservoir at the end of East King Street and from there it flowed by gravity through wooden mains to the center of the city. For the rest of the century the water continued to be supplied untreated, resulting in numerous diseases. The volunteer fire companies were able to connect to hydrants, however, and the threat of serious fires was reduced.

As the city's population increased, more streets were built. With the increase in residents social problems such as crime, public immorality, and lack of care for the mentally ill became concerns of a small but vocal minority of city folk. The city fathers were more concerned with market standholders cheating their customers and young men racing their horses and carriages through the dusty streets.

In the 1840s illuminating gas was manufactured from rosin and piped through the streets to bring light to streets, public buildings, and the homes of the wealthier citizens. A telegraph line connected Lancaster to the outside world. Newspaper publishing seemed to be a major activity, with every political party and faction putting out its

James Buchanan was Pennsylvania's only native son U.S. president. "Gentleman Jim" or "Old Buck" also was the only bachelor president. Aristocratic, highly intelligent, ambitious, and exceedingly cautious, Buchanan revered the law and the Constitution more than popular adulation. He died in Lancaster in 1868.

own newspaper. The venerable *Intelligencer* continued to be the main organ of the regular Democrats. The Anti-Masonic and Whig Party published its own paper that was merged into the *Examiner* and eventually became the Republican organ. As many as 10 other sheets were issued during campaigns. Newspapers "took off the gloves" when it came to politics and used tactics that would be shocking even in modern times.

The political complexion of Lancaster during the 19th century was curious. Although the surrounding county always remained firmly dedicated to conservative politics, the city's major parties were more evenly divided between the Democratic Party and their various opponents (National Republicans, Anti-Masons, Whigs, Native American "Know Nothings," and Republicans). Prior to the Civil War the local democracy had two major factions: one headed by former Federalist James Buchanan and another based in Philadelphia, headed by George Dallas. After the Civil War Republicans were more successful in winning city offices.

Lancaster was home to a number of nationally famous politicians during the 19th century. James Buchanan became a lawyer in Lancaster in 1812 and won elections as a Federalist to the state legislature, then to the U.S. House of Representatives, where, as chairman of the House Judiciary Committee, he almost singlehandedly saved the federal judiciary, including the Supreme Court, from being destroyed by states rights advocates. As a conservative pro-Constitution Democrat, Buchanan served in the U.S. Senate, as secretary of state under President Polk when the territory of the nation was increased greatly, as minister to Great Britain, and as president of the United States during an impossible "no-win" period of history. He died in Lancaster at his beloved *Wheatland* in 1868.

Thaddeus Stevens, a native

Thaddeus Stevens served as U.S. Representative from Lancaster County from 1859 until his death in 1868. He served in the Pennsylvania House of Representatives 1833–1835, 1837, and 1841. In 1842 he moved to Lancaster and established a law office. Stevens was known as the "Father of the Free School Act" in Pennsylvania and the "Father of the Reconstruction Act" in Congress.

of Vermont, moved to Lancaster from Adams County in 1841 and set up his law practice here. He was elected to Congress on the Anti-Masonic slate, then as a Whig and as a Republican. Stevens was the most vigorous and outspoken foe of slavery in Congress. After the Civil War he was regarded as the "Father of Reconstruction" and he managed the impeachment of President Andrew Johnson.

Simon Cameron was born in Maytown, Lancaster County, to an impoverished Scottish family. Through his ambition and intelligence Cameron became a successful and wealthy canal and railroad contractor, printer, and banker. He served in the U.S. Senate, as minister to Russia, and as Secretary of War in Lincoln's first cabinet. He returned to the U.S. Senate where he served until 1877, when he resigned in favor of his son, Donald. Both Camerons were leaders of the Republican Party.

A flurry of building activity occurred in Lancaster in the late 1840s and early 1850s. The face of Lancaster was changed with the building of a vast cotton mill complex, a new prison, and a new courthouse. Many city churches put up new buildings or modernized old ones.

Lancaster's banks came into existence at the urging of the town government in 1803, when the body invited the Bank of Pennsylvania to establish a branch office. In 1810 the Farmers Bank of Lancaster was organized, and today it has evolved by merger into the National Central Bank. During the chaotic days of early banking the Farmers Bank was characterized by conservative action, where caution tempered any inclination to speculate or take unnecessary risks. In 1814 the bank was chartered by the state, giving it the distinction of being the first home-owed bank in Lancaster. These early banks issued their own notes for use as currency, and they invested in other banks and enter-

East King Street in 1858 was a sea of mud in wet weather and quite dusty at other times. Duke Street crosses in the middle of the photo. At the left side, above Duke Street, was a favorite stopping place for stagecoaches to county towns as well as to Philadelphia and other cities. Reigart's Old Wine Store is now the site of the Provident Book Store, Christian booksellers.

prises. The state also purchased heavy quantities of stock in the banks, giving the state partial ownership as a major shareholder.

The panic of 1837 prompted the city to issue money called *skinplasters.* Lancaster's close control over the currency avoided many of the problems encountered elsewhere where the temptation to abuse the issuance of "homemade" notes was given free rein. Even the city redeemed its loan with fractional currency in 1838. These came in denominations of 10 cents, 12 1/2 cents, 25 cents, and 50 cents. The prevalent use of 12 1/2 cents in those days came from circulation of Spanish pieces of eight, eight of which amounted to one dollar.

In 1841 the Lancaster County Bank was founded and, like the Farmers Bank, it benefited from prudent directing. Never in its history has the bank's integrity or stability been placed in any danger.

The banking needs of the city also were met by a half-dozen private bankers such as Gyger and Company, Reed McGrann and Company, and A.S. Henderson.

Christopher Hager, merchant and civic leader, in 1852 built Fulton Hall, now known as the Fulton Opera House.

In 1855 the Lancaster Philharmonic Society presented its first concert, but an alarm of fire in the town emptied the hall during the violin arrangement of the *casta diva* from Bellini's *Norma.* Members of the Union Fire Company and their ladies were in attendance, evidenced by the unseemly but obligatory departure during a cultural high point. The philharmonic's repertoire was heavy on overtures to Italian operas, Gyrowetz's symphonies, and marches by the orchestra's own conductor, Maestro Keffer.

Another entertainment, the Lancaster circus, advertised "the most Grand, Rich and Rare Collection of Living Animals ever exhibited in America." Lancastrians were treated to the sights of two Arabian camels, one of each sex; a "real Red African Lion, almost full grown...and the keeper will kiss him," an African ape, and llamas from Peru, among other oddities.

On College Hill, once known as Gallows Hill where murderers were executed by hanging, Franklin and Marshall College took shape in 1853. Franklin College, a preparatory academy for young German-speaking gentlemen, had been functioning in Lancaster under the watchful eyes of the Lutheran and German Reformed churches since 1787. At Mercersburg, the college named for John Marshall, chief justice of the Supreme Court from 1801 to 1835, was controlled by the German Reformed Church. The two institutions were combined under the direction of the German Reformed Church. Old Main and two identical flanking buildings, all of red brick and sandstone Gothic Revival architecture, were dedicated in 1857. The college, one of the oldest liberal arts colleges in the nation, has had a long and distinguished history in higher education.

At nearby Millersville the proposed Lancaster County Academy became in 1855 the commonwealth's first teacher-training school. Its faculty included some of the most illustrious names in American education. Now, as Millersville University, it is both a liberal arts college and a professional training school.

The Lancaster Business College was founded in 1855 and trained local students in business for 135 years. Preparing ministers for the German Reformed Church since 1871, the venerable Lancaster Theological Seminary now trains ministers for all churches, and is known for the excellence of its instruction and its legacy as heir to the enlightened tradition of German scholarship.

Lancaster's children were being educated in public schools as early as 1809, if their parents did not mind being classed as paupers. By 1822 all children were to be educated at public expense in Lancaster. Even earlier, advocates of the teaching methods of Joseph Lancaster practiced their art in the city. In 1834 the common school system was introduced, which provided an education for all, regardless of wealth and station in life. Lancaster's early schools were barrackslike structures often built in series along the streets. African-American students were educated in a separate building. A night school functioned as early as 1840.

Lancaster experienced a rapid growth in population in the 1840s. Efforts were made to provide adult education for Lancaster's mechanics and laborers who grew up in an era where public education was not available. All manner of public forums and lycea were established to educate those who wished to improve their economic and social conditions.

Emigrants from Ireland and Germany flocked to Lancaster to work in the industries. A surplus of young women supplied the labor market in the cotton mills. Low wages and long hours (six to six) were the rule. The city's large middle-class population continued to thrive while the immigrants struggled—often successfully—to climb the ladder of upward mobility.

To pipe water into Lancaster city, this water-pumping plant was built in 1837 along the Conestoga River downstream from East King Street. Originally the pumps were powered by waterwheels. Later, steam engines were added and a boiler house was built. The water was forced up to reservoirs along King Street at Franklin Street.

Although not one of Lancaster's more desirable addresses, the Lancaster County Prison on East King Street has presented an imposing appearance since 1847. John Haviland was the architect.

A lithograph shows Lancaster's first textile mill about 1829. The mill was located on the west bank of the Conestoga River just south of the Duke Street Bridge.

Built in 1852, Lancaster's Fulton Opera House was designed by architect Samuel Sloane, who also designed the new court house and Victorian modifications of Trinity Lutheran Church. It was first used as a meeting hall, then was reconstructed as a theater in 1873. The historic structure welcomed all the great actors, actresses, and entertainers of the late 1800s and early 1900s. Still in use as a theater today, the Fulton continues to undergo restoration.

CHAPTER THREE

The Rise of Communities

An 1848 painting of the Susquehanna River at Chiques Rock shows the Haldeman Mansion at the left and the second Columbia Bridge in the distance. The original painting by Frederick DeBourg Richards is owned by the Heritage Center of Lancaster County.

The first communities in Lancaster County grew around intersections of major roads. At these places were to be found a grist mill for grinding grain into flour and meal and an inn for the refreshment of travelers, which also served as the community's social center. Early road petitions documented the necessity for a road to a certain mill. Mills were powered by water and therefore were located along streams. Very early in its history Lancaster County had many mills scattered along its streams. Transportation over unpaved roads was difficult. Because few bridges existed most of the streams were crossed by fording.

The Conestoga wagon was the 18-wheeler truck of the 18th and 19th centuries. Created in the Conestoga Valley of Lancaster County, this wagon was a large, sturdy vehicle shaped like a boat to prevent cargo from shifting. Despite its massive wheels with wide rims, the Conestoga wagon was graceful and colorful. With a blue body, red undercarriage, and white cloth cover, the wagon, drawn by teams of four or six powerful horses, hame bells jingling, was quite a sight.

The roads to Philadelphia and New Castle, Delaware, were lined with wagons hauling barrels of flour, casks of whisky, furs, hides, lime, and hemp. On their return to Lancaster County communities, the wagons brought to the country general stores articles the local settlers could not make for themselves.

Some Lancaster citizens had become well-to-do and wished to provide their homes with fine furnishings. Philadelphia merchants sent glassware, furniture, silks and fine fabrics, books, and imported goods. Local artisans produced those articles that required special skills. Most farmers had a skill in addition to farming. Some were blacksmiths, weavers, cabinetmakers, wheelwrights, potters, gunsmiths, or tinsmiths.

Flour milling was the most important industry in Lancaster County during the 18th and much of the 19th centuries. The county's nearly 300 grist mills produced thousands of barrels of flour. In addition to wheat, early Lancaster County farmers grew rye, barley, and corn (maize). Some of these grains were used to distill whisky. About one-quarter of the local farms had stills.

Other mills also were constructed at an early date. These included clover mills, oil mills (to press linseed oil from flax), paper mills, and saw mills. All were operated by water power.

The abundance of iron ore and forests (for charcoal production) made Lancaster County a center of

The Grubbs and Haldemans mined iron ore for their blast furnaces from this pit in West Hempfield Township. Eventually filled with water, the pit became known as Lake Grubb. Other smaller pits were located along the Marietta Pike and local miners lived in the areas of Ironville and Silver Spring.

iron manufacture in the 18th and 19th centuries.

Blast furnaces constructed in the northern and southern parts of the county produced pig iron from ore, charcoal, and limestone. Air was forced into the fiery furnace stacks by bellows or blowing tubes operated by waterwheels. Forges were built along county streams.

Waterwheels provided the power to lift the heavy forge hammers that formed heated iron into bars, plates, and rods. For more than a century rural Lancaster County resounded to the thump-thump-thump of forge hammers. Night skies glowed red from furnace fires.

As the population increased and communities grew larger, the general store and the blacksmith shop appeared. After a dozen or more houses were built in the vicinity, a church was erected. Sometimes the church was a structure used by several congregations until each denomination had sufficient members and funds to erect its own building.

In the northern part of Lancaster County German Reformed and Lutheran congregations often built union churches in which the Reformed congregation would worship one Sunday and the Lutheran the next. Eventually most union churches dissolved, with each congregation having its own structure.

Those early Lancaster County churches that required an educated ministry—Reformed, Lutheran, Moravian, Presbyterian, and Episcopalian—established schools or academies in connection with their churches. They emphasized classical languages, history, geography, mathematics, and moral philosophy.

The young men that graduated from Lancaster County academies usually went on to fine colleges and universities where they studied for the ministry, law, or medicine.

Built in 1854, Eagle, or Chickies Furnace No. 2, was one of a row of eight anthracite iron blast furnaces located between Marietta and Columbia near the Susquehanna River. Production of pig iron was a major industry in Lancaster County prior to 1900. The engine house in the center of this 1889 picture is still standing.

The academy associated with the Chestnut Level Presbyterian Church was especially distinguished for the excellence of its teaching and the success of its graduates. Another early school was connected to the Moravian community at Lititz. It, too, is renowned for its excellence. The academy at Marietta was noted for the quality of its teachers, some of whom went on to outstanding careers as college and university professors and presidents.

People require goods. As communities grew, more trades and occupations were needed. Shops making shoes, tinware, furniture, clocks, barrels, wagons, carriages, and hardware appeared in the villages.

Larger villages had volunteer fire companies, militia companies, musical bands, and a town hall where lectures would be given. By the middle of the 19th century most towns had a lyceum or hall where debates, lectures, theatrical entertainments, and civic meetings were held. Inasmuch as public education had begun after most young adults started rearing their families, adult education for young adult males helped reduce illiteracy and encouraged many to develop their intellectual curiosity.

Prosperous citizens established libraries and reading rooms in the 1840s and 1850s for "mechanics" that wished to better themselves through education. Traveling "professors" journeyed around Lancaster County communities lecturing on all manner of subjects, from phrenology to experimental chemistry. Enterprising physicians lectured to the public on anatomy and diseases, with due regard for the morbidly curious by describing two-headed infants and other abnormalities.

Clergymen jumped into the rush for higher learning by explaining ancient history and classical civilization. Not to be outdone, female lecturers assaulted the male monopoly by asserting that women have brains, skills, and rights, too. Such

The Conestoga wagon of local invention and construction was the heavy-freight hauler of the 18th and 19th centuries. Its broad iron tires rumbled over Lancaster streets carrying goods to Philadelphia and to the West. The boat-like shape of the body was designed to keep freight from shifting on hills.

Rein's Dutch Mill in Earl Township was built in 1793, replacing a log mill erected by Theodorus Eby in 1717–1719. During the American Revolution, millers George and John Rein were caught selling barrels of flour to the British. The mill was later owned by the Green Bank Mill and then by Roland's Mill. The facility had two waterwheels, two sets of millstones, and was fairly typical of the nearly 300 grist mills in Lancaster County that produced flour and meal from various grains.

The Zion Lutheran Church, pictured here circa 1905, was established around 1825. Suspended over the altar in oversized letters is Martin Luther's famous phrase, "A mighty fortress is our God."

exhortations generally were expressed in the more sophisticated communities where heresies were tolerated or where there were bound to be a goodly number of Lancaster County Quakers present.

Lancaster County represented both extremes in its appreciation of education and cultivation of intellectual qualities. Public education was opposed vigorously by two groups: those who could afford to send their children to private or church academies and those who regarded education as unnecessary.

At the other extreme were leading advocates of public education, persons such as Thomas Burrowes of Strasburg, who was the "Father of Pennsylvania Public Education," and Thaddeus Stevens, "Savior of Pennsylvania Public Education." Both were Lancaster lawyers and political leaders. An English visitor to Lancaster wrote, "That among all the Colonies, [he] did not visit a more cultured town than Lancaster."

In an agricultural paradise the invention and refinement of farm machinery would be expected. Lancaster County's ingenious farmer-mechanics turned their talents to increasing production and lightening the burden of farming almost as soon as the forests were cleared. As early as 1806 a threshing machine was erected at David Witmer's mill that could thresh and clean 100 bushels of wheat in eight hours. Joseph Fawkes of Bart Township in 1859 invented and built a steam plow that earned him prizes at country fairs. Unfortunately his plow was more suited to the heavy prairie sod of the Midwest than to the soils of Lancaster County.

Jacob Mowrer secured a patent in 1869 for a double corn shovel harrow, and his teen-age son, Nathaniel, invented a corncob crusher as well as a device for extracting the eye out of corn before grinding.

The youthful Joseph Shirk of East Earl Township developed an improved scythe and cradle that was many times more efficient than the traditional implement. From the inventive minds of local farmers

Lancaster County was dotted with one-room schoolhouses, such as this one in Manheim Township on Pleasure Road. Schoolmaster George Hambright and his scholars posed for this picture in 1877.

grew many county foundries and machine works that eventually culminated in the huge internationally recognized Ford New Holland plant.

Every community of any size had institutions that furnished protection, enlightenment, entertainment, and financial stability. Throughout much of the 19th century virtually every borough and large village had at least one bank. Lancaster County bankers take pride in their conservatism and their careful investing of their depositors' funds. Despite these recognized virtues, many banks in Lancaster city and county were forced to close during the Depression of 1931–1933.

In a rural area with far-flung farms, firefighting is of prime importance. Lightning and spontaneous combustion are ever-present dangers. Every village in the late 19th century tried to have some firefighting organization. Usually the apparatus was a primitive hand pump on a small wagon. Larger boroughs had more advanced pumpers and hose carriages; around 1895 to 1905 a few large boroughs had steam fire pumpers drawn by manpower or horses and early in the 20th century chemical wagons often were used.

It was not until the 1920s, however, that county towns began forming volunteer fire companies equipped with motorized apparatus capable of responding to farm fires. Now more than 84 volunteer fire companies, equipped with the most advanced equipment including powerful pumpers, aerial trucks, tankers, rescue trucks, and hazardous materials trucks, safeguard rural Lancaster County. The local fire company is an important institution in each community and membership carries prestige.

During the 19th century every village seemed to have a band

Philip Lebzelter, a German immigrant, founded the Eagle Wheel and Bending Works in Lancaster in 1854. This plant became the largest establishment of its kind in Lancaster, and it included hardwood tree lands. When rubber tires were invented, Lebzelter became a Goodyear distributor, and today the firm, now owned by John Way, is the oldest Goodyear distributor in the nation. This photo of the Lebzelter employees was taken about 1892.

Emanuel Shober's Eagle Hotel, located at the northwest corner of North Queen and West Orange streets, was in operation for most of the 19th century. Later known as the Columbian, this venerable downtown Lancaster hotel was demolished in 1890 to make way for a YMCA building.

Captain Thomas Thurlow, chief engineer of the Union Fire Co. No. 1, stands beside his steamer about 1870. Captain Thurlow's trousers were gray, his shirt green, and the numeral "1" gold. His belt was green and gold.

or at least a small brass ensemble or cornet band. In some communities such as Ironville, the band was comprised mostly of members of two or three families that furnished a dozen or more musicians. On a warm summer evening the community bandstand could be counted upon to fill the air with marches, waltzes, and ballads. Many band musicians were veterans of Union Army unit bands.

Today two or three community bands continue to provide music for Lancaster Countians.

Lancaster's letter carriers in the late 1890s were more mindful of the U.S. Postal Service slogan concerning rain, sleet, and snow when they reached newly opened streets with calf-high mud. This photo was taken on the steps of the Lancaster Post Office, now the City Hall.

Their members come from many communities and musicianship is of the highest quality.

Before insurance companies began selling life and health insurance policies in any great numbers, the family breadwinner looked to the numerous beneficial societies to provide for his family in case of tragedy. Beneficial societies had fanciful names and included entrance rituals borrowed from what was believed to be Masonic practice.

Many county communities had branches of these societies: United Ancient Order of Druids, Ancient Order of Good Fellows, Improved Order of Red Men, Junior Sons of America, United Order of American Mechanics, Knights of Pythias, Patriotic Order of Sons of America, Independent Order of Good Templars, Sons of Temperance, Knights of the Mystic Chain, and the Independent Order of Seven Wise Men, to name a few. Each society embraced both patriotic and religious principles. The Independent Order of Odd Fellows had many lodges throughout the city and rural communities.

Other community organizations included the Patrons of Husbandry, or Grange, which was a family-oriented society with rituals that appealed primarily to rural folk; and various German societies (Verein) and singing groups, such as the Maennerchor and the Liederkranz, which kept alive in vigorous form the culture of the Old Country.

The women had societies dedicated to such virtues as temperance, chastity, and family life. Charity and benevolence were the objectives of many such societies.

Lancaster's Iroquois Band takes time out to pose in front of the old Foltz Building on East Chestnut Street, about 1916. This band was one of Lancaster's best, in an era when parades and outdoor ceremonies demanded the most of skilled musicians.

The Ancient and Honorable Order of Free and Accepted Masons, the oldest of the fraternal groups, had lodges in Lancaster County as early as 1755. The earliest surviving lodge is No. 43 located in Lancaster since 1785. Two other lodges are in the city and nine other Masonic lodges are in county towns today. Appendant bodies of the Freemasons function in Lancaster and Columbia. The proprietor of Lancaster, James Hamilton, was Grand Master of the Pennsylvania Masons; and President James Buchanan was Master of Lodge No. 43 in the city.

The Masonic Homes operated by the R. W. Grand Lodge of Pennsylvania began in 1910 at Elizabethtown and today the vast complex provides retirement facilities.

Expanded many times over the years to accommodate more people and provide the most modern residential and health care, the facility is one of the finest of its kind in the nation. The stone buildings, chapel, Grand Lodge Hall, health care and hospital structures are situated amidst formal gardens that are in bloom much of the year. The Homes' farms provide produce, meat, poultry, fruit, and berries for the residents. Adjacent to the campus of the Masonic Homes is the Pennsylvania Youth Foundation through which the Grand Lodge helps youth prepare to accept the challenges of tomorrow.

Named in honor of the civil engineer who built the Conestoga Navigation Canal, Edward Gay, the steamboat Lady Gay *plied the Conestoga River giving pleasure to the young people of the late 19th and early 20th centuries.*

Zeamer's Drug Store in 1900 was one of Columbia's cherished institutions. Its soda fountain was elegant and equipped to dispense all kinds of beverages and ice cream treats.

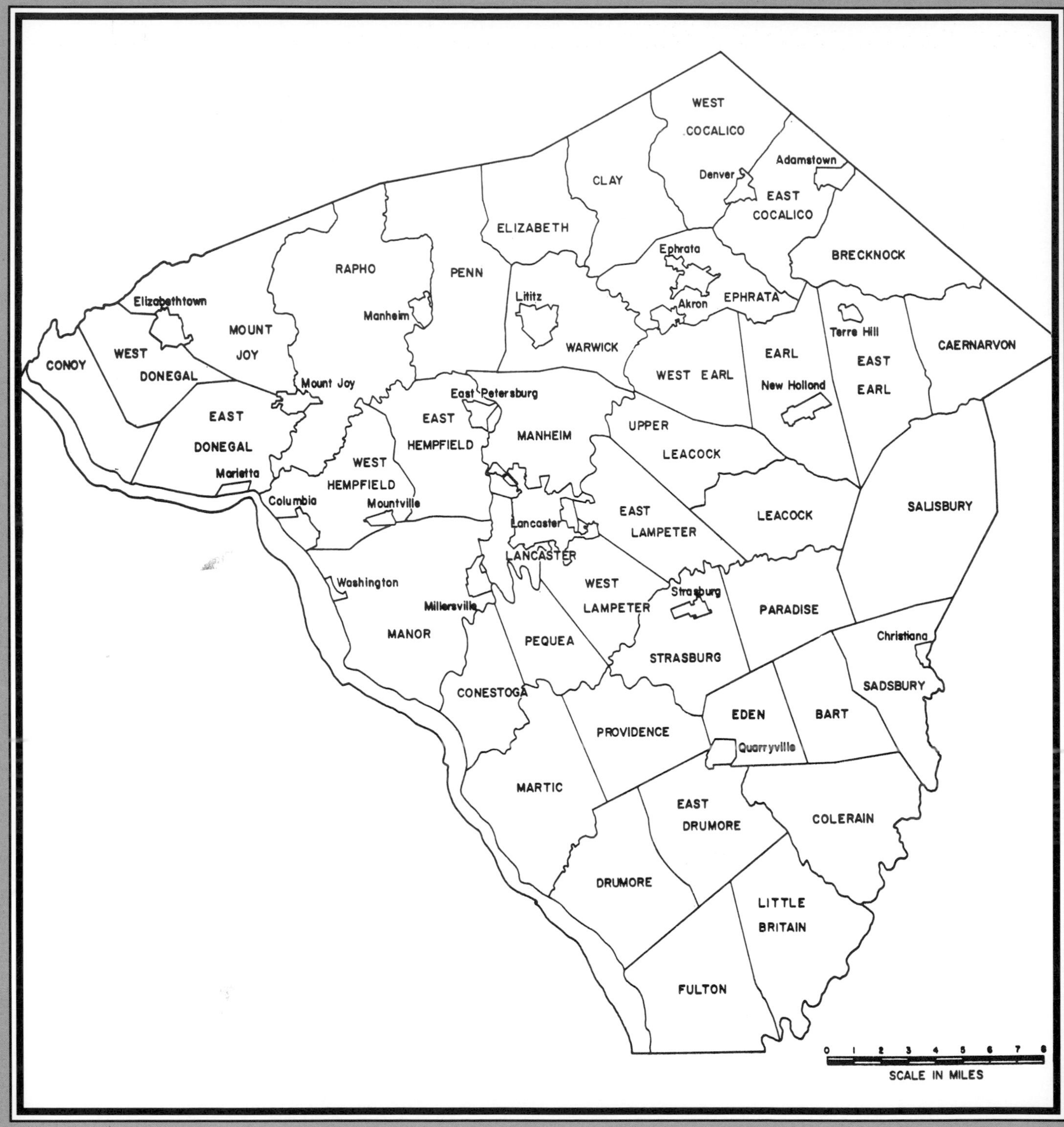
WEST COCALICO
CLAY
Denver
Adamstown
EAST COCALICO
ELIZABETH
BRECKNOCK
RAPHO
PENN
Ephrata
EPHRATA
Akron
Lititz
Elizabethtown
Manheim
Terre Hill
MOUNT JOY
WARWICK
CAERNARVON
CONOY
WEST DONEGAL
EARL
EAST EARL
WEST EARL
New Holland
Mount Joy
East Petersburg
EAST DONEGAL
EAST HEMPFIELD
MANHEIM
UPPER LEACOCK
WEST HEMPFIELD
Marietta
Columbia
Mountville
SALISBURY
LEACOCK
Lancaster
EAST LAMPETER
LANCASTER
Washington
WEST LAMPETER
Strasburg
PARADISE
Millersville
MANOR
PEQUEA
Christiana
STRASBURG
SADSBURY
CONESTOGA
EDEN
BART
PROVIDENCE
Quarryville
MARTIC
COLERAIN
EAST DRUMORE
DRUMORE
LITTLE BRITAIN
FULTON
0 1 2 3 4 5 6 7 8
SCALE IN MILES

C H A P T E R F O U R

County Boroughs

Established in 1729, Lancaster County now comprises 941 square miles. It borders York County on the west, Dauphin and Lebanon counties on the north, Reading County on the northeast, Chester County on the southeast, and Cecil County, Maryland, on the south.

The appearance of Lancaster County has changed significantly over the centuries since the days when the early settlers cleared areas in the wilderness for their farms. The changes were not as apparent throughout the 19th century. Forests disappeared and many more farms dotted the countryside. Hamlets and villages sprang up. But until the end of the 19th century, the county remained bucolic and unspoiled by urban development. Three developments in particular changed the landscape and the quality of life most Lancaster Countians profess to cherish. The principal and very human cause for change has been the desire of people to live outside the city in a rural setting, where more space, fresh air, and personal freedom are likely to be found. To accomplish this, suburbs developed, and continued to expand into the countryside. Even the older boroughs became too crowded, and they, too, became centers around which suburbs developed.

Facilitating such development were two other factors: transportation and public utilities. With the development of street cars, or electric trolleys, and later, motor cars and trucks, movement between the city's factories, offices, cultural activities, and homes in the country was expedited. Eventually factories and offices moved out into the countryside. Water and sewer lines extending into the countryside encouraged increased development. With the gradual urbanization of the suburbs have come the less fortunate aspects of living: higher taxes, rising crime rate, traffic congestion, and the disappearance of the beautiful farmland and its the way of life. These developments need not ruin the countryside if they are planned to preserve the beauty and quality of life in Lancaster County. The Lancaster County Planning Commission works heroically to bring order out of chaos through intelligent planning while keeping the human dimension foremost.

When communities were settled is a question that confounds historians. What is the founding date—the arrival of the first inhabitants, the purchase of the first tract of land? It may be said the 1710 Herr settlement east of Willow Street was the first permanent settlement of European immigrants in the county. This early settlement remained rural. Other settlements grew into boroughs with substantial population.

Columbia

When Robert Barber, John Wright, and Samuel Blunston settled along the Susquehanna River in 1726, those Chester County

The watch industry began in Lancaster in 1874 with the Adams and Perry firm. After five bankruptcies the Hamilton Watch Company emerged in 1892, and is pictured here in 1904. Becoming the renowned "watch of railroad accuracy," Hamilton pioneered many technological developments, including the electronic watch.

Below: Operating under state control by 1834, the Pennsylvania Canal carried freight and passengers between Pittsburgh and Columbia. This canal boat at Collins Station in Conoy Township was typical of the vessels that carried such bulk freight as coal, ore, and lumber.

Quakers already had made political names for themselves. John Wright became Lancaster County's first "president of the court" in 1729, and to him fell the honor of naming the new county. Barber became the first sheriff and Blunston was appointed the first prothonotary-recorder-registrar.

In 1730 John Wright received a patent to operate a ferry across the broad river. Thenceforth the community was known as Wright's Ferry rather than Shawnee Indian Town. John Wright's extraordinarily gifted daughter, Susannah, easily was one of the most brilliant citizens in the American colonies. She possessed a mind that grasped and applied the teachings of science, philosophy, law, medicine, linguistics, and politics. Her friends and correspondents included Benjamin Franklin, David Rittenhouse, and the members of the American Philosophical Society. Susannah died unmarried but earlier she had inherited the large estate of Samuel Blunston with whom, it is said, she had a platonic relationship. When Susannah died in 1785, aged 84 years, she left her estate to her nephew, Samuel, son of James Wright.

Samuel Wright was eager to develop Wright's Ferry into a bustling town. In 1788 he laid out 160 lots to start his town and renamed the community Columbia. He hoped the name would be helpful in his effort to have Columbia made the national capital. That would have succeeded but for one vote. Columbia also tried to become the state capital.

As Irish, Germans, Welsh, and other ethnic groups settled in the town, churches were built for their worship. Two Roman Catholic parishes were established and churches for the German Reformed, Lutheran, Methodist, Presbyterian, and Episcopalian congregations were built. Other denominations arrived later. The Quaker meeting began as early as 1738.

With Quaker benevolence encouraging them, free black persons and some runaway slaves settled in Columbia early in its history. Stephen Smith and William Whipper became prosperous lumber merchants. Smith was one of the first black philanthropists in the nation.

Columbians were proud of their schools and the Washington Institute. Two newspapers flourished. Educational and cultural

Front Street in Columbia was a bustling center of commerce in the 1800s. Railroad trains competed with horse-drawn wagons and pedestrians along the busy street that paralleled the Susquehanna River. In this 1873 view, the colonnaded American House offered accommodations to overnight travelers.

events brought crowds of people to the stately French Empire Opera House which, when built in 1874, was one of the finest and largest structures in Lancaster County. Its auditorium was said to have acoustical qualities found only in Philadelphia's Academy of Music. Men and women in the arts and literature were at home in Columbia. Lloyd Mifflin, claimed as America's greatest sonneteer, was both poet and artist. Reginald Wright Kauffman, journalist and author, wrote dozens of books and covered the activities of peace conferences and the old League of Nations for the *New York Herald-Tribune.* During World War I he was a war correspondent who sent back his dispatches from the front lines. Although Columbia was well-supplied with lecturers, artists, musicians, and entertainers from its midst, the outstanding theatrical road companies always stopped at the opera house.

Columbia's economy depended upon its location along the river. As Wright's Ferry, the town earned the name Gateway to the West. When the Pennsylvania State Works, a system of canals, inclined planes, and a railroad, were built in 1830 to 1834, the eastern terminus of the canal was at Columbia. The Columbia and Philadelphia Railroad, as it was originally called, connected Philadelphia to the canal. The entire system was designed to feed the products of western and central Pennsylvania to the eastern market, and especially to Philadelphia.

Marylanders were not pleased with this development because Baltimore liked to believe it was the natural market for western Pennsylvania commodities. Investors in Maryland and the Susquehanna Valley formed the Susquehanna and Tidewater Canal Company in 1840 to siphon off cargoes from canal traffic at Columbia and divert it across the river to Wrightsville then down their canal along the west shore of the river to Havre de Grace, Maryland, and on to Baltimore. Less than a decade later the Pennsylvania Railroad acquired the Pennsylvania State Works. Through interconnections the railroad was able to do what canals were unable to accomplish. Although the canal from Clark's Ferry above Harrisburg to Columbia continued to carry heavy bulk commodities until the end of the 19th century, the bustling canal basin at Columbia gradually declined in favor of the railroads.

Columbia was a railroad center. It was served by five rail-

A Pennsylvania Railroad 12-wheeler en route to Lancaster with two boxcars crosses the high stone bridge over the Conestoga River in 1895. The bridge, built in 1888, was left unfinished on its south side so that it could be widened to accommodate more tracks, although they were never needed.

In the early 19th century, Peter McTague's Seven Stars Saloon on Columbia's Front Street was favored by hard-drinking raftsmen and canal boat crews. Although some decay was well-advanced by the end of the century, adjacent residences show evidence of fashionable early years.

roads during the 19th and early 20th centuries. The Columbia and Philadelphia Railroad, after 1847 known as the Pennsylvania Railroad, entered Columbia and ran along an inclined plane. Trains of cars were pulled up the plane by a stationary steam engine. In 1840 the plane was taken out of service and a more efficient route was built from the Centerville Road to Columbia. The original route closely followed the present Route 30.

A separate railroad corporation, the Harrisburg, Portsmouth, Mountjoy, and Lancaster Railroad Company, was constructed from Harrisburg to Lancaster where it connected with the railroad to Philadelphia. A branch was built from Royalton near Middletown (Portsmouth) to Columbia, following the east bank of the river.

Another group of Maryland investors decided a railroad from Baltimore directly to the Pennsylvania canal system at Harrisburg would be beneficial to Baltimore's economic interests. The Baltimore and Susquehanna Railroad Company then built a line from Baltimore to York and on to Harrisburg. Eventually this railroad went north to New York State and was known as the Northern Central Railroad. At York a line was constructed to Wrightsville and across the covered bridge into Columbia.

Philadelphia's economic chiefs were furious. It seemed every effort put forth by Philadelphia to have Pennsylvania's commerce directed to their city was thwarted by the Baltimore interests. Persons living in the lower Susquehanna Valley profited from the rivalry between the two great seaport cities. Under the Pennsylvania Railroad's auspices the Columbia and Port Deposit Railroad was built in 1877. It linked Columbia to Perryville, Maryland, and to the Pennsylvania's subsidiary, the Philadelphia, Wilmington, and Baltimore Railroad mainline. All these railroads came under the control of the Pennsylvania Railroad system.

To local manufacturers the need for anthracite coal and a means of transporting freight to and from northeastern Pennsylvania's industrial districts resulted in chartering the Reading and Columbia Railroad in 1857. Construction was delayed by the Civil War but soon after the struggle ended, the railroad was completed from Columbia to Sinking Spring near Reading where it joined tracks of the Philadelphia and Reading Railway Company.

A fine depot designed by Frank Furness was built at the southeast corner of Locust and Bank streets in Columbia. In 1905 the Pennsylvania Railroad built a low-grade freight line from Atglen to Enola, the tracks running through Columbia. By 1910 Columbia began to see the decline of its reputation as a railroad town. It became a whistle stop and hundreds of jobs were lost. The Pennsylvania Railroad operated a large roundhouse where locomotives were maintained. Before long all these facilities were gone. Today only the Royalton Branch, the Columbia-Port Deposit line, and the Columbia Secondary track (the original section of the state railroad) are in operation.

During the 1840s Colum-

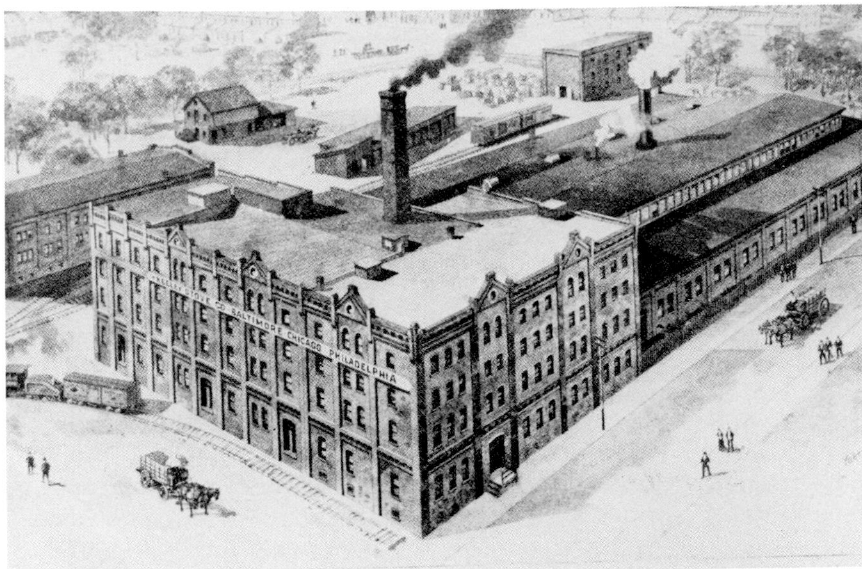

The sprawling Keeley Stove Works at Second and Maple streets in Columbia produced hundreds of thousands of cast iron cook stoves, ranges, and parlor stoves between 1882 and 1948.

bia became a center for anthracite iron furnaces and rolling mills. The canal and railroads facilitated the transportation of coal, iron ore, and limestone to the furnaces, and shipment of pig iron and wrought iron shapes from Columbia. Silk mills and a lace mill provided employment for hundreds of workers. Many small foundries produced iron castings for the railroad and industrial trade. The Keeley Stove Works manufactured cook stoves and parlor stoves that were found in homes across the nation.

In 1814 Columbia was incorporated as Lancaster County's third borough. During the War Between the States, Columbia found itself in the uncomfortable position of being Lancaster County's first line of defense. As General John Brown Gordon's seasoned Georgia troops marched eastward from York, Lancaster County was thrown into panic. Rumors abounded: the rebels would burn Columbia and Lancaster. Major elements of the Union army were far away. Wrightsville was to be defended and fortifications were thrown up at Columbia. The Georgians made short work of invading Wrightsville and started into the covered bridge across the river in pursuit of the fleeing defenders. In the center of the mile-long wooden bridge attempts were made to blow up the span. That didn't work, so a committee of Columbia's leaders—there must have been thousands of them according to their proud descendants—set an oil car afire and sent it and its blazing cargo into the bridge. Flames roared through the wooden structure and drove the erstwhile invaders back to Wrightsville. A few days later the Battle of Gettysburg was fought. Columbia was saved!

Columbia has a proud tradition of furnishing excellent military leaders to the U.S. Army. Major General Edward C. Shannon

On June 28, 1863, Lancaster Countians were alarmed when General John Brown Gordon's Georgian troops started across the Columbia bridge preparatory . It was set afire, driving the Confederates back to York County.

(1870–1946) and Lieutenant General Daniel Bursk Strickler (1897–1992) were two of the most outstanding military men; both also served as lieutenant governors of Pennsylvania.

With the dawn of the 20th century, Columbia faced many challenges to its economic future. The iron industry became technologically obsolete and the canal no longer was used. The textile industry moved out and was followed by the closure of the huge stove works. The people were not discouraged, however, and small industries continued to operate successfully. A large foundry for manufacturing pipe fittings was built in the 1920s and now functions as the Grinnell plant.

Ephrata

The borough of Ephrata was incorporated in 1891, but the first settlers arrived in 1732 as followers of Johann Conrad Beissel. Beissel left the Dunker Brethren after a dispute with Alexander Mack and established his monastic community at Ephrata, a scriptural term meaning "fruitful." Convents were built, mills were erected, and three orders of inhabitants were organized: a sisterhood, a brotherhood, and the congregation of married householders. They worshipped on the seventh day, or Saturday. After the revolutionary war, during which time cloister buildings were used as hospitals for wounded soldiers, and the death of Beissel, the community declined and eventually ceased except for a small number of householders who came under the care of the Seventh Day German Baptist Church. The cloister complex now is administered as a museum by the Pennsylvania Historical and Museum Commission.

During the 19th century Ephrata became the market center of northeastern Lancaster County. The Reading and Columbia Railroad

The Ephrata Cloister was established in 1724 by Johann Conrad Beissel, following a break with the Dunker Brethren. This 1900 view of the cloister shows the Saal or House of Worship (upper left) and the Bethania or Brother's House (far right).

served the community. Ephrata benefited from its favorable location at the junction of the Lancaster-Reading Road and the Paxtang Road. Numerous cigar factories and businesses serving the surrounding farmland prospered. Modern Ephrata is one of the principal boroughs of Lancaster County. It supports various educational and cultural activities and maintains a first-rate 150-bed hospital.

Strasburg

Incorporated in 1816, Strasburg was settled as early as 1750 or possibly earlier. Named for the French-German city, Strasburg, the village also had a nickname, Bettle Housen, the German dialect term for "beggars' houses." Apparently the first houses were not very elegant. Among the settlers were a number of Huguenot families. The Old Conestoga Road ran through the village, facilitating its growth. Today Strasburg has many fine old homes that are well-preserved by their owners.

At one time in the 1830s a railroad track ran down Main Street before turning northward to the Pennsylvania Railroad. The cars were drawn by horses until the 1850s when the present Strasburg Railroad was constructed and fitted out with a steam locomotive. Strasburg has remained a rural town with few small industries, which suits the residents fine.

Education always has played a prominent role in Strasburg. Thomas Burrowes, father of Pennsylvania's public school system, lived in Strasburg. The town's academic life was centered in its Strasburg Philosophical Society (1790), the Classical Academy of John Whiteside (1796), and the Strasburg Scientific Society (1791). An unverified tradition states that Dr. Joseph Priestley, the British Unitarian

The Red Rose County

Lancaster is known as the Red Rose County. In England the Wars of the Roses occurred from 1452 to 1471. The struggle was between the House of Lancaster, headed by Henry VI, and the House of York, led by Richard, Duke of York, and later by his son, Edward IV. The red rose was the symbol of the House of Lancaster. The House of York used the white rose as its mark. Ironically, neither the Duchy of Lancaster (Lancashire) nor the Duchy of York (Yorkshire) used the roses as emblems; they were the personal symbols of the royal houses.

Lancaster County, Pennsylvania, was named by John Wright to honor his birthplace in England. The red rose did not become a trademark for Lancaster until 1907 when the sponsor of the Jamestown, Virginia Exposition requested Lancaster to send a flag and the red-faced local officials discovered Lancaster did not have one. Frank Reid Diffenderffer, former president of the Lancaster County Historical Society, the Honorable Benjamin Champneys Atlee, and Samuel M. Sener designed the flag with its red rose. Fred P. Mentzer put the design in proper artistic form, which then was executed by the Horstmann Flag Company. Beneath the stylized red rose and seal is a natural red rose on its stem. The seal includes the Penn arms, a Conestoga wagon, and three sheaves of wheat.

The red rose has an earlier association with Lancaster County. When the famed glassmaker-ironmaster, Henry William Stiegel, gave the Lutheran congregation in Manheim a lot on which to build its church, he stipulated that one red rose shall be paid annually as ground rent. Consequently, the church is known as the Red Rose Church and the annual payment to a Stiegel heir is a colorful event each June. Thus this delicate flower of rare beauty has come to symbolize Lancaster.

Adjacent Counties

When Lancaster County was erected May 10, 1729, its western and northern limits were not defined. For many years, the Kittochtinny-Blue Mountain range, which stretches in a northeastern direction from Franklin County to northern Berks County, marked the limits of expansion as the number of settlements increased.

New townships were formed by action of the Lancaster County Court and when the population boom required it, new counties were formed from Lancaster County.

York–1749
Hallam, Chanceford, Dover, Manchester, Manheim, Monaghan, Paradise, Shrewsbury, Warrington, Cumberland, Hamiltonban, Straban, Tyrone, Menallen

Cumberland–1750
Hopewell, Pennsborough, Antrim, Lurgan

Berks–1752
Bethel, Bern, Brecknock, Caernarvon, Cumru, Robeson, Heidelberg, Tulpehocken

Northumberland–1772

Dauphin–1785
Derry, Paxtang, Londonderry, Hanover, Lebanon

Lebanon–1813
Lebanon, Heidelberg

minister and chemist who discovered oxygen, lived for a short time in Strasburg in the 1790s. The Strasburg Railroad, now a prospering tourist attraction, and the adjacent Railroad Museum of Pennsylvania, bring large numbers of visitors to Strasburg.

Marietta

Marietta, like its neighbor, Columbia, is a river town. Settled as early as 1715 by Scottish Presbyterians, the location was known as Anderson's Ferry. James Anderson, Jr. was the son of the Donegal Presbyterian minister and he established the ferry. In 1804 James Anderson IV laid out the town of Waterford. He disposed of the lots by lottery, charging $60. Adjacent land was laid out in lots by David Cook who named his town New Haven. The two developers did not bring their street grid into harmony and to this day the disjointed streets add a perverse charm to Marietta. Later, Jacob Grosh developed his addition at the eastern end of town, and named it Moraviantown. Cynics named it "Bungletown." At the western end of Marietta is Irishtown, laid out by John Pedan, James Mehaffey, and James Duffy in 1813. With individuality characteristic of the Scots and the Irish, streets in Irishtown ignore the grid of adjoining Waterford. Irishtown was in East Donegal Township until it was annexed to Marietta in the late 1960s. Marietta was incorporated as a borough on March 6, 1812, becoming the second oldest borough incorporated in Lancaster County. With the incorporation, Waterford and New Haven ceased being separate entities.

A strong civic spirit manifested itself in the community. A market house was built, an excellent school was established, and a church for the use of all fledgling congregations was erected. A bank and numerous small industries added greatly to the town's economy. The Pennsylvania Canal flowed through Marietta between Front Street and the Susquehanna River. Lumber rafts on the river were broken up at Marietta where large saw mills produced millions of feet of lumber for shipment to the eastern markets. When the frozen river thawed in the spring of each year, the rafts with their colorful crews arrived at Marietta and the town saloons thrived—always a time for fathers to warn their daughters to stay away from the raftsmen.

In the 1840s, when the lower Susquehanna Valley prospered on anthracite iron production, Marietta shared with Columbia the distinction of being the Pittsburgh of the East. Eleven anthracite iron blast furnaces operated between Marietta and Columbia. Later in the 19th century a large hollowware foundry was constructed for the manufacture of cast iron and enameled vessels. Cigar factories, breweries, and the famous vaccine farm and laboratory were other local industries. Modern Marietta offers employment to persons working in the local foundries, ceiling tile, pharmaceutical manufacturing, and grain storage businesses.

During the 1870s everyone important in the nation—U.S. presidents, senators, industrialists, leading politicians, governors, publishers—arrived in Marietta in their private railroad cars to visit with Colonel James Duffy whose hospitality was lavished upon his important guests. After sumptuous dinners followed by brandy and cigars, the guests decided who would be nominated for national and state offices.

Pride in Marietta's heritage flowered in the 1960s when residents took steps to preserve their town and its many early 19th-century houses. With leadership provided by the Marietta Restoration Assoc-

Colonel James Duffy, a jovial cattle dealer, contractor, and friend of the politically powerful during the Gilded Age, built this High Victorian mansion in Marietta. Maintained in good condition by its present owner, the mansion still stands, though without its original porch.

iates, the town museum/school and the Union Meeting House were restored. Marietta had the good fortune to be excluded when the automobile began the destruction of charming old communities. Much of Marietta now is within a historic district designation. Many fine old mansions of the ironmasters and lumber mill owners are preserved.

Mount Joy

Originally consisting of several villages, Mount Joy was incorporated as a borough February 10, 1851. The name chosen by its developer, Jacob Rohrer, derived from the ship *Mount Joy*, which honored the English General Mountjoy who was a hero in the eyes of Ulstermen. The ship played an important role in the struggle between the Protestants and Catholics of Ireland.

Rohrer sold his 134 lots by lottery for $85 per ticket. The center of this community is the square formed by East Main and High streets. Since this was in 1812 at the height of land speculation, Rohrer was obliged to dispose of his lots over the next 27 years, taking much reduced prices. Richland was the name of the community at the intersection of New Haven and Manheim streets with West Main Street. This village consisted of 122 lots, all sold within one year.

Another village was started by Christian Cohick in 1830; it was laid out between Marietta Avenue and Delta Street and was called Mount Joy Continued. When Jacob Wallick bought land in the vicinity of Manheim and Old Market streets in the 1830s, he called his community by the cumbersome name Richland and Mount Joy Connected. Other extensions to the town received names no longer used. In

The grounds of the Lancaster County Agricultural Fair were along the Harrisburg Pike in Manheim Township, now the site of the R. R. Donnelley printing plant. The county fair was discontinued in the early 1930s because its managers felt that sideshows of questionable morality compromised the integrity of the fair and because numerous county communities held fairs of their own. Several of these community fairs, such as Solanco and Lempeter, continue to be strictly agricultural and focus on rural family life rather than a carnival atmosphere.

the mid-20th century the village of Florin was annexed to Mount Joy borough.

When the Harrisburg, Portsmouth, Mountjoy and Lancaster Railroad was built in 1834, the line went through Mount Joy. A railroad car manufacturing factory was built along the tracks, as were several foundries and other industries.

Philip Frank erected a large malting house on Market Street at the railroad. Alois Bube operated a brewery nearby. Other industries in Mount Joy included shoe factories, farm implement works, cigar factories, the Brady Edge Tool Works (whose axes Abraham Lincoln preferred), Brown Textile Mills, a food processing machinery company, flour mill, and more recently, electronics components and chocolate manufacturing.

Mount Joy was the site of several noteworthy schools of the 19th century. The Cedar Hill Female Seminary operated between 1836 and 1864, educating many young ladies in the classical tradition. Rosters show that girls from 11 states, many of them in the South, were boarded and educated at the seminary. Horsemanship and boating were in the curriculum. The Mount Joy Institute for Boys was started under Scottish Presbyterian sponsorship about 1838. Another Scottish school for boys was opened in 1851 as Moore's Academy. This school closed during the Civil War and later the structure became the Mount Joy Soldiers' Orphans School. There were 35 soldiers' orphans schools established but the one at Mount Joy was regarded as the most successful owing to the high quality of supervision. As many as 400 students were accommodated at one time. Their ages ranged from seven to 16 and the boys and girls wore uniforms. In 1890 all the schools were closed except the Scotland School in Franklin County. The Richland Academy also functioned in Mount Joy prior to the acceptance of public education.

Clarence Schock was a 20th-century benefactor of Mount Joy. He established the Schock Independent Oil Company (SICO) late in the 19th century. It prospered and Schock shared his profits with numerous community and church organizations. He was especially interested in education and all the profits of the petroleum distributing firm go to the SICO Foundation, which administers the granting of college scholarships to thousands of high school graduates in the service area of the company. It now includes southeastern Pennsylvania, Delaware, and part of New Jersey.

Elizabethtown

Chartered in 1872, Elizabethtown has grown to be one of Lancaster County's largest boroughs.

Its origin was in the purchase of land in 1753 by Barnabas Hughes, a tavern keeper. Tradition claims Hughes named his community to honor his wife, Elizabeth. Located along the Harrisburg Turnpike about 18 miles from Harrisburg, Lancaster, and Lebanon, the community prospered by caring for the frequent travelers in its several inns. Merchants of various commodities and supplies opened stores. Blacksmiths, wheelwrights, carpenters, wagonbuilders, and other artisans found Elizabethtown a fine place to pursue their trades.

The Harrisburg, Portsmouth, Mountjoy and Lancaster Railroad was constructed in 1834 along the western edge of Elizabethtown. The railroad served as a stimulus to local industry. During the 19th century various foundries and mills operated in the community. In 1893 the Church of the Brethren founded Elizabethtown College, a liberal arts college. A large chocolate-processing plant is a major employer in Elizabethtown today. Earlier in the 20th century two large shoe manufacturing plants and a farm machinery works were the major industries.

Elizabethtown borough has numerous churches to provide for the spiritual welfare of its citizens.

Manheim

The borough of Manheim was incorporated May 16, 1838, but the town was laid out by Henry William Stiegel, the colorful ironmaster and glassmaker, in 1762. Situated along a road from Lancaster to Lebanon, the community was populated by German immigrants and their families. The main street was Charlotte Street but soon after its founding the principal street was Prussian Street, which retained its name until the war hysteria of 1917 when the name was changed without imagination to Main Street. A large Market Square was located between Prussian and Charlotte streets with High Street on an east-west axis through Market Square—the largest public square in Lancaster County.

Stiegel built his mansion at the northeast corner of Prussian and East High streets. It is said he tried to live as lavishly as a German baron and therefore was called Baron Stiegel. Despite his love of high living, Stiegel was a devout Lutheran churchman and a congenial gentleman who looked after the welfare of his employees with genuine care. He owned a charcoal iron furnace (Elizabeth Furnace) near Brickerville. With characteristic energy he built a glass manufacturing plant at Manheim where his employees made glass that today is highly prized and exceedingly rare. As the revolutionary war clouds gathered, the "Baron" became insolvent and spent the rest of his life in the employ of others as a clerk and schoolmaster. When Manheim was laid out, Stiegel donated a lot on which to build a Lutheran Church. His only payment was "one red rose to be paid annually to himself or his heirs." After Stiegel's death late in the 18th century the presentation

The Black Bear Inn was a landmark at Elizabethtown as early as 1733. A son of Barnabas Hughes, who laid out Elizabethtown, kept the tavern for many years.

A panoramic drawing presents the prosperous McGwann mansion and farm in Manheim Township along New Holland Pike. Early farms were known as plantations.

ceremony was discontinued. In 1892—more than a century ago—the ceremony was resumed, with leading members of the bench and bar, historians, and political leaders presenting addresses on Stiegel and his contributions to humankind.

Throughout its history, Manheim has been a center of commerce for northern Lancaster County, serving the rural population of Rapho and Penn townships. The predominantly German character of the borough with its busy merchants and tradesmen enabled the town to prosper. Its location along the Chikiswalungo Creek ("Big Chickies") made the community a prime industrial site for mills. In the 20th century the borough's industries have been a large machine and foundry works, a sprawling plant for the manufacture of asbestos textiles and friction materials such as a clutch facings and brake linings; a foundry and works for producing wheels and castors; a factory for making belting; and several textile and garment factories.

The Reading and Columbia Railroad served the community, and its restored depot is the headquarters of the very active Manheim Historical Society. Perhaps harkening back to the days when Manheim's artisans and mechanics demonstrated a singular know-how, many of the town's citizens demonstrate a fascination for things mechanical.

Lititz

Lititz was a Moravian settlement from the 1740s to 1855, when non-Moravians were able to pur-

Displayed in a walnut Dutch cupboard dating to the 1760s, this extraordinary collection of Stiegel-type glass is from the same time period. Stiegel was a maker of fine glass just prior to the American Revolution and products of his Manheim glassworks are extremely rare.

chase property in the community. Warwick was north of the Reading and Columbia Railroad and Lititz was south of the tracks. The original name was Litiz, a corruption, it is said, of the Czech village of Lidice.

The Moravian community was centered around its church and all members were expected to conduct their lives in accordance with church regulations. Many skilled artisans practiced their trades and art and music were encouraged.

Education was important to the Moravians so schools were started upon the founding of the settlement.Linden Hall Seminary for girls was founded by the Moravians in 1794 and continues today as a fine boarding preparatory school. The Moravians were a tolerant peace-loving people, and their presence contributed greatly to the heritage of Lancaster County.

During the 19th century Lititz saw the formation of various small industries facilitated by the railroad. Tobacco processing, furniture manufacturing, and several agricultural implement foundries prospered. The Sturgis pretzel bakery, still in existence, is thought to be the oldest pretzel bakery surviving in the nation. Modern Lititz has a major chocolate producer and is the location of the Warner-Lambert Pharmaceutical Company, makers of Listerine.

Long ago Warwick was absorbed into Lititz and the community was incorporated as a borough in 1888. Lititz is an exceptionally clean and civically progressive place and its residents have pride in their community.

Akron

Akron (Greek for "high place") was known as New Berlin when a handful of settlers established the community on a hilltop southwest of Ephrata. The arrival of the Reading and Columbia Railroad in 1863 required building a station that was called Akron Station. The mail train carried mail to residents in New Berlin but it had to be addressed to Akron Station. During the latter part of the 19th century the name New Berlin passed into history and Akron took its place. In 1895 the borough of Akron was incorporated. Aside from the usual rural tradesmen, Akron's major industry was shoe manufacturing. Akron is so close to Ephrata that its history in large part is that of Ephrata. Modern Akron's principal industry is pure, clear bottled water.

Denver

Known early as Bucher Thal (Bucher Valley), the community took on the name of Union from its inn of that name. When the Reading and Columbia Railroad was built through the town in 1863 and the railroad company established a station, the stop was called Reamstown Station. The community of Reamstown is some distance south of Denver and is not along the railroad. This confusing situation resulted in Reamstown Station being changed to Union Station and in 1881, to Denver. Denver was incorporated as a borough in 1900.

Located between East and West Cocalico townships, the community served as a rural economic center for those townships. Inns and general stores provided for the populace. Several flour mills and a distillery were the early industries. Until the dawn of the present century, the Pennsylvania-German dialect was used almost exclusively in the area. The dialect is also known as Pennsylvania Dutch, a corruption of the German word

The mid-18th century Moravian Community of Lititz was remarkable for its craftsmen and the quality of its art and music. Located in a historical district, the Moravian buildings form a charming complex of incredible beauty. Built in 1787, the Lititz Moravian Church was gutted by fire in 1957 but it has since been restored with great accuracy.

In 1750 the Moravian congregation of Lancaster built a stone church along Market Street near West Orange Street. This structure was torn away in 1820 when the congregation built a large brick church.

"Deutsch," which means "German."

Many small businesses, including the famed Leisey coverlet weaving shop, prospered in early Denver. The town's location along the Lancaster-Tulpehocken Road aided the development of Denver. As in many northern Lancaster County communities, numerous cigar factories flourished. Modern Denver became home to several textile mills, a shoe company, and a hat company. A large nationally recognized bakery and a major distribution center of the Woolworth chain operate at Denver.

Adamstown

In 1761 William Addams laid out a town that he named Addamsburry. Its position along the Lancaster to Reading Road encouraged the establishment of inns and facilities to care for horses, stagecoaches, and travelers. When the electric trolley railway to Adamstown was built in 1905, its transfer station with the Reading electric cars was the Lancaster County House, one of the principal hotels. From the 1890s a steam locomotive drew the passenger car from Mohnton to Adamstown. At Mohnton passengers could transfer to the Reading electric trolley system. It was possible for Lancastrians to travel to Reading by train or by trolley.

Early industries in Adamstown were tanneries, distilleries, cigar factories, and hosiery mills. Wool felt hats were made by several firms following the Civil War. Modern Adamstown's major employer is the George Bollman Hat Company, manufacturer of standard headgear, top hats, cowboy hats, and high quality novelty hats. Antique shops attract visitors. The town was incorporated as a borough in 1850. The community is progressive and benefits from the civic liberality of the Bollman Company.

Terre Hill

Terre Hill began as a small village in East Earl Township after a group of settlers were attracted to a country church and school in the 1830s. The hamlet came to be known as Fairville but when a post office was requested in the late 1840s, the name of Fairville already was used for a post office in Chester County. Since the village was on a hill, the name Terre Hill (earth hill) was adopted. In 1900 the village was incorporated as a borough.

Somewhat remote from any major highways, the town sustained the general stores and other institutions necessary for the population. A school and several churches supplied educational and spiritual enlightenment. The major industries were cigar factories. In more recent times the economy has been maintained by several garment factories and concrete products works.

New Holland

One of Lancaster County's larger boroughs, New Holland had its origin as a village in Earl Township in 1760. In that year Michael Diffenderffer planned a development laid out in 25 lots. Earlier settlers with characteristic individuality ignored the planned streets and the intentions of Diffenderffer. The residents knew the place as Earltown, but soon it was called New Design, which may have had something to do with the haphazard sitting of homes and streets. By the 1770s the name New Holland came into use. The village was incorporated as a borough in 1895. Located along the much-travelled road from Lancaster to the Downingtown-Harrisburg Turnpike at Blue Ball, and the French Creek district, New Holland became the principal town in Earl Township. The Reformed and Lutheran churches were built early in the town's history. Other churches followed soon afterward.

Many of Lancaster County's early prominent leaders settled in Earl Township and their descendants also took their places in the governmental, judicial, educational, and political life of this county. The first Anti-Masonic newspaper in the county was published in New Holland in 1829. Thomas Edwards was an early justice of the county court. Nathaniel Ellmaker was a state senator, and John Kittera served in the U.S. Congress. Amos Ellmaker, state assemblyman, district attorney, and justice of the court in Dauphin County, was the vice-presidential candidate on the Anti-Masonic ticket in 1832. William Hiester was a candidate for Congress in opposition to James Buchanan; later, as a Whig, he won a seat in Congress. Anthony E. Roberts also served in Congress after being sheriff of Lancaster County. Isaac Hiester served in Congress and numerous other persons from the New Holland area filled the state legislative and county offices.

The railroad from Lancaster to Downingtown ran through New Holland, which encouraged the location of small industries. One such industry, a farm machinery works, grew into the vast industrial complex, Ford New Holland, which manufactures leading-edge agricultural machinery for worldwide distribution. Modern New Holland is a progressive borough with excellent schools, numerous churches, and various cultural activities.

Christiana

Christiana has the dubious honor of being the most "forgotten" borough in the county, owing to its remoteness from Lancaster city. Christiana is on the Chester County line and was incorporated in 1894 as a borough. This pleasant little borough lies along that narrow corridor of southeastern townships that were settled by the English and Scots. The Germanic culture that pervades much of Lancaster County was absent from Christiana until

Nolt's Mill in Warwick Township, on Lititz Creek, provided an idyllic backdrop for this earnest young man fishing with a seine in the 1880s. Only a small portion of the graceful old bridge remains and the mill is long gone, having been burned in 1900.

The Leacock Friends Meeting House at Bird-in-Hand was constructed in 1790 and served those Quakers of the Lampeter-Leacock vicinity who were active in helping slaves escape via one of four underground railroad routes that passed through Lancaster County.

recent times. Amish carriages now are seen in and around Christiana. The old State Works Railroad, later the Pennsylvania Railroad, runs through Christiana. The town was taken from Sadsbury Township, originally part of Chester County.

Many of its earliest settlers were Quakers. The Pine and Octorara creeks join at Christiana and form a stream that powered numerous mills and forges in the 19th century. Students in Christiana and Sadsbury Township attend school in Chester County.

Industries that took form along the railroad and Octorara Creek included foundries, machine shops, and railroad repair shops. A major industry is the venerable Christiana Machine Company, manufacturer of water turbines and other cast and machined products.

In 1851, not far from Christiana there occurred a "riot" caused by a Maryland slaveholder accompanied by friends and a posse led by a deputy U.S. marshal that came to reclaim two fugitive slaves. The slaves, aided by other fugitive and free black persons, put up vigorous resistance, and the slaveholder was killed and his son badly wounded.

Local citizens who arrived on the scene were requested to assist the marshal in carrying out the provisions of the Fugitive Slave Act, but they refused and were arrested for treason. A trial was held at Independence Hall with Thaddeus Stevens defending the 38 neighbors who refused to assist the marshal. After a series of trials in federal and county courts, all defendants were found not guilty. With that the Christiana Riot became a footnote in history and a harbinger of what was to come a decade later.

Quarryville

The borough of Quarryville was incorporated in 1892 and its citizens observed its centennial in ancient form, complete with the growing of beards. The community of Quarryville began as a settlement around and near Barr's limestone quarry. Limestone was quarried extensively in southern Lancaster County, with much of it burned in lime kilns. Used mostly for agricultural purposes, much of it was shipped to Philadelphia and Newport, Delaware. A very old stone building, called "The Ark," is situated near the major quarry and remains today as the first, and still surviving, structure in Quarryville. It is said to have been built in 1791. Early in the 19th century a settlement grew around Barr's quarry. Hotels became an attraction and the community was the social and economic center of southern Lancaster County. About 1837 an attempt was made to establish a post office, but that did not materialize until 1849. Southern Lancaster County has dozens of hamlets but Quarryville is the only major community. It is the site of a true agricultural fair each September. Dairying is an important business in the Quarryville area.

In the 1870s a railroad was built from Lancaster to Quarryville. The Quarryville depot also was a terminal of the Quarryville spur of the Lancaster, Oxford and Southern Railroad, a narrow gauge line that connected Peach Bottom on the Columbia and Port Deposit Railroad with Oxford on the Pennsylvania Railroad's Philadelphia and Baltimore Central Branch. The railroad, affectionately known as the "Little, Old, and Slow," was an agricultural line that served the farmers of southern Lancaster County. A passenger car generally was included in each train and many tales have been told of the train patiently waiting for farm folk to cross fields to board the car. When the low-grade freight railroad was constructed in 1905–1907 by the Pennsylvania Railroad, it ran adjacent to the northern boundary of Quarryville. When the Quarryville branch was abandoned in 1973 a siding from the low grade was provided to serve Quarryville industries. With the abandonment of the low-grade railroad, Quarryville no longer has a rail connection to the outside world.

Although the Amish have spread into southern Lancaster County, the English and Scottish families that have descended from the early settlers still constitute a significant part of the population. Friends' meetinghouses and Presbyterian kirks are to be found in the area, as are many other churches.

Mountville

Located along the old Lancaster-Columbia Turnpike, Mountville was known first by its earliest Pennsylvania-German settlers as "Sich Dich Fore" or "look ahead." As with most settlements along a road, an inn, the Black Bear, was the local center of activity. In 1814 Isaac Rohrer, a land speculator, laid out 130 lots that he proposed to sell in a lottery for $140 per lot. Rohrer named his community Mount Pleasant owing to its high elevation. Rohrer reserved Lot No. 1 for himself and on it he built a home for his family and a hotel. The hotel has survived to this day. It was called the Stock Exchange Hotel in the late 19th century and is the Mountville Inn today.

Rohrer also set aside at the west end of his tract two lots for a public schoolhouse and a public meetinghouse which was used as a nondenominational church for fledgling congregations not ready to erect their own churches. Debates, lectures, and entertainments were held in the building in the middle of the 19th century. This structure was abandoned when the present town hall used by the VFW was constructed.

An unusually progressive town, Mountville had excellent schools and organizations devoted to civic improvement, adult education, and cultural events. It was on the Columbia branch of the Pennsylvania Railroad, which facilitated travel to and from Mountville. The 1834 original railroad from Columbia to Lancaster and Philadelphia ran north of Mountville on the site of Orkney Road, but after 1842 it followed the present route south of Main Street. When the post office was established in 1842, the name

Before the advent of cars and buses, towns and villages not situated along railroad and trolley lines were served by stagecoach. This 1902 photograph shows the Intercourse stage on its way from Spring Garden to Lancaster. Its daily Lancaster stop was at the Sign of the Leopard at 105 East King Street.

George W. Hensel, also known as the "Sage of Quarryville," was a man who enjoyed life thoroughly, commented on the passing scene, wrote sophisticated newspaper columns, and was a gentle satirist. By occupation a hardware merchant and by avocation a rural philanthropist, writer, and counselor to the multitude, Hensel conceived and organized the Slumbering Groundhog Lodge of Quarryville, a group of gentlemen dedicated to the proposition that wit and humor are the leavening of civilization. Every Groundhog (or Candlemas) Day brings out the lodge members in top hats and white gowns for a day of fun and spoofing.

Mountville replaced Mount Pleasant.

Industries in Mountville were a large brickyard; cigar factories and tobacco warehouses; a wallpaper printing plant; and a wood products company, which manufactured cedar chests and other products. The Fridy Machine Company turned out hoists and machines that enabled one man to position freight cars on sidings. The Mountville Manufacturing Company, known locally as the plow works, was a foundry and machine company that produced many kinds of agricultural implements, troughs, and castings used in other industries.

Modern Mountville's industries include a large plant of Ford New Holland. A mile east of the borough is the Hempfield Industrial Park containing many industries and businesses. Mountville was incorporated as a borough in 1906.

Millersville

First called Millersburg and Millerstown, the community was laid out by John Miller, a blacksmith, in 1761. The lots were five acres each with Miller receiving ground rents. Growth was slow. The usual store, inns, and tradesmen were scattered among the homes, some of which dated to before the American Revolution. In 1820 the post office was established.

Rural Lancaster County held much hostility toward education. Many, but certainly not all, of the Germanic population saw no need for schooling. Even when the Pennsylvania Public Education Act of 1834 was passed, many rural districts resisted or ignored the act. When obliged to establish schools, some districts, with militant reluctance, provided minimum facilities with incompetent teachers—whatever could be obtained at the least cost. Enlightened citizens, including many of German background, tried to remedy that condition without much success. As a result, private academies were established. One such school was the Millersville Academy. Despite the efforts of its supporters, obtaining financing was drawn out, but in 1854 a building had been erected.

That same year Dr. James Pyle Wickersham had been appointed superintendent of Lancaster County Schools. L. M. Hobbs, a teacher from New York state, and Wickersham were of the opinion teachers were poorly prepared. They decided to hold Teacher Institutes in the county. The success of these programs led Wickersham and Hobbs to take over the academy as a teacher-training institution. Thus was born the Millersville Normal Institute, which evolved into the First State Normal School at Millersville. After 1861 the state legislature aided the school with appropriations and in 1917 the Commonwealth of Pennsylvania purchased the school outright. In 1927 Millersville State Teachers College was authorized to grant degrees and operate as a regular four-year college. Later, with the addition of liberal arts courses and authorization to offer graduate courses and degrees, the school became Millersville State College.

In 1983 the state-owned colleges became universities and today Millersville University is a large sprawling complex of buildings and nearly 8,000 students. The University has a downtown campus in Lancaster and working arrangements with several local hospitals in offering courses in medical technology and bachelor degrees for graduate nurses.

The absence of any local industry has made Millersville a bedroom community. In 1875 Lancaster's first horse car line ran between the Pennsylvania Railroad depot and Millersville to transport the normal school students. Although served by frequent bus service, Millersville finds itself a victim of too many motor cars and too few high-volume streets and highways. Millersville was incorporated as a borough in 1932.

East Petersburg

The youngest borough in Lancaster County, East Petersburg was incorporated in 1946. Its strategic location at the intersection of the Lancaster-Lebanon Road and Old Peter's Road called for an inn and facilities for travelers. In old histories the community was named for Peter Bezaillion, an old Indian trader whose trail passed by the place. Daniel Wolfe, a local merchant, laid out 79 building lots that sold quickly during the land speculation fever of 1812.

Not much happened to Petersburg until after the Civil War when the Lancaster branch of the Reading and Columbia Railroad was built not far from the town. Slowly the community expanded toward the railroad. The designation "East" apparently was added to Petersburg when the post office was established. The northwestern section of the community was called "Heckel Stettle" by the rural folk.

As suburban Lancaster crawled northward after World War II, little area was left between East Petersburg and the suburban development and industrial parks. In time East Petersburg may become an enclave in suburbia.

The Christiana Machine Company, a manufacturer of turbines, gearing, and power transmission equipment, has been a major industry for more than 130 years.

The Power of Industry

Workers at the old match factory at Safe Harbor in Conestoga Township lined up for this photograph sometime in the 1890s. It was a good source of employment for many area residents, including numerous youngsters, who started working at the age of 12.

The mid-19th century saw Lancaster County change from an agricultural economy with virtually no large industry except for a few charcoal iron blast furnaces, to a predominantly agricultural economy with diverse but small industries. Many of these industries were farm-related such as tanneries, leather-processing, lime-burning, and agricultural implement manufacturing. Flour milling continued to be the county's first ranked industry in capital investment and value of product.

With growing industrialization, especially in the city, serious economic problems were aggravated by unemployment, inflation, speculation, and chaotic banking. Lancaster County mirrored the economic conditions of the nation, but less so.

During this period the first generation of industrial enterprise began, providing jobs for men and women and encouraging new immigrants to settle among the old residents. Despite the general lack of sophistication and technological know-how, Lancaster saw trade unions and industries develop, first stumbling, then enthusiastic, and finally maturing into workable, practical instruments for a healthy economy. Then, as later, the salvation of Lancaster County's economy was its diversification.

As war clouds gathered in late 1860, Lancaster Countians had greatly differing emotions. The "plain folk" were opposed to war and merchants enjoyed good trade with the South. The Republicans were opposed to slavery and its extension into the new states that were being created. The local democracy was torn between neutrality and "pro-North" sentiment. Few in Lancaster County had anything good to say about slavery.

Lancaster's own President James Buchanan soon would be retiring from the White House and returning to his beloved *Wheatland.* When the Civil War began, Lancaster County's men signed up for military duty. County towns offered bounties to enlistees.

A strong group of "Copperheads" (Democrats loyal to the South) from the northeastern section of the county rioted when they were called up in the draft. Local industries and farmers once more produced for the war effort. As in most places some manufacturers and cattle dealers made fortunes supplying the Union Army. Patriotism was very much in fashion and anyone who did not conform paid the penalty.

On the first day of the Battle of Gettysburg, Lancaster's Major General John Fulton Reynolds was killed. Rosina Hubley, Lancaster's "one-person" Red Cross and USO,

Long after the famed Pennsylvania rifle was developed in Lancaster County in the mid-18th century, Henry Eichholtz Leman was proprietor of Lancaster's largest gunworks. Leman guns and rifles were shipped far and wide; many western hunters carried Leman weapons.

An 1861 drawing shows Lancaster women making uniforms for Union soldiers. It was reproduced in Harper's *magazine.*

organized the Patriot Daughters who rolled bandages, nursed the sick and wounded, and raised money by holding "Sanitary Fairs." When the war ended and the citizen-soldiers returned home, many on crutches or minus limbs, the Lancaster Countians greeted them as heroes. Hundreds of homes in Lancaster County mourned the loss of loved ones.

With Reconstruction underway, Lancaster's Congressman, Thaddeus Stevens, was generating headlines nationally with his verbal assaults on the slave-owners of the South, and his demands for severe punishment for the white South. He thought Lincoln's philosophy of "charity for all and malice toward none" was wrong, but his real wrath was turned on Lincoln's successor, President Andrew Johnson.

Constables kept the peace in Lancaster from the beginning, and by 1865 the police force consisted of 10 uniformed constables and a special detail of 20 men called "night police." In 1867, when the charter was updated, a police department was established and staffed with seven officers for the nine wards. Councilmen played politics with the appointments, a sorry situation that lasted to 1925. In 1874 the first police station was built on Grant Street behind First Reformed Church and the lock-up moved there from the basement of Old City Hall on the square.

Strangers had difficulty finding addresses, so an ordinance was adopted in 1871 that established a numbering system. The ordinance mentions "Centre or Penn Square," the first official use of the name recognized today.

As the centennial of American independence approached, the city councilmen believed Old City Hall on the square, with its classic Georgian architecture, was hardly representative of the modern and bustling city. Bids were sought to demolish the structure, but replacement costs were too great to erect a Victorian monstrosity to house the city government. Later, the Masonic Lodge urged the city to cooperate with the lodge in removing Old City Hall and the equally handsome lodge hall, both to be replaced with a Victorian building. Again the city could not afford to tear down the historic and handsome buildings.

Lancastrians in 1876 talked about the big affair in Philadelphia, the Centennial Exposition. School pupils prepared artwork, penmanship, and other samples of their achievements for display. Local industries and farms sorted over their best examples for exhibition at Philadelphia. Lancaster walked off with many prizes and ribbons.

The Lancaster City Gas Company supplied gas to illuminate houses and businesses. In 1876 another gasworks was built by the Lancaster Gaslight and Fuel Company, and three years later the two companies merged. Organized in Lancaster in 1886, the Edison Electric Illuminating Company fur-

nished the first electrical power in the city. Smarting under the competition, the Lancaster County Gaslight and Fuel Company bought the Edison company and combined operations. In 1900 control of the stock of the gas company passed to the Lancaster County Railway and Light Company, which, in turn, was acquired in 1926 by the Lehigh Power Securities Corporation.

A city ordinance required the power company to paint its poles white. The location of poles often was a serious political matter, and property owners occasionally extorted fat sums of money from the electric company for the privilege of planting poles. Street gas lamps gradually gave way to overhead arc lights.

By the end of the 19th century Lancaster was in full swing in its second generation of industrial development. The Penn Iron Works was rolling bar iron; half a dozen lock companies produced many thousands of padlocks and other hardware; umbrella factories, including the famed Follmer and Clogg Company, largest umbrella factory in the world, seemed determined to protect the whole earth from raindrops; and carriage manufacturers rolled their buggies and wagons off the assembly lines in a steady parade of vehicles.

Lancaster's breweries by then were called the Munich of the West and the beer was shipped as far as Boston to satisfy discriminating taste. The highly diversified industries turned out corks, combs, leather, furniture, watches, cigars, steam engines, cotton goods, and even microscopes. A center of the cigar industry, the city had factories and tobacco warehouses covering many acres and employing hundreds of women and children. Watches had been made in Lancaster in a factory predating the Hamilton Watch Company from the mid-1870s.

Labor unions kept pace with the development of industry. Among the trade unions were the ironworkers, weavers, brewers, cigarmakers railroad employees, carpenters, printers and typesetters, foundry workers, and painters. A series of wage demands by the cigarmakers' union eventually caused the proprietors to move their operations from Lancaster, thus ending a major local industry.

Horsecar transportation from Lancaster's railroad station at North Queen and East Chestnut streets to Millersville began in the mid-1870s and by 1890 the city streetcar lines were operated by electrical power. All trolley lines ended at the square in Lancaster, then the hub of commerce in Lancaster County. Salesmen from Lancaster wholesale houses took advantage of the trolleys to visit merchants in the towns, making them aware of the latest goods the city merchants were offering. During the next two decades electric trolley lines were constructed to outlying parts of the county.

Large Victorian mansions sprang up along North Duke Street

Major General John Fulton Reynolds, son of a prominent Lancaster family, lost his life on the first day of the Battle of Gettysburg, but only after personally placing his units where they would be able to withstand the Confederate offensive.

Many drummer boys that served during the War Between the States were only 14 or 15 years old. One of the experienced local drummers was Israel C. Landis, who joined the Union Army to train combat soldiers.

The second block of North Queen Street with the Orange Street intersection in the foreground is shown about 1888. The poles were laden with telephone wires.

in Lancaster and dotted the countryside as prosperous farmers and merchants showed off their wealth. By the 1880s, downtown merchants retained a lively concern in the appearance of their shops.

The early 19th-century storefronts, with windows of many panes, had begun to look dowdy, so new facades replete with every Victorian gimcrack known to architects were built. The entire south side of the first block of East King Street went Victorian in 1883. Gaslights hissed and glowed where oil lamps so recently had smoked and sent out dim illumination.

The "Gilded Age" had come to Lancaster County with a flourish! Fine carriages drawn by sleek matched horses moved smartly along the streets as their owners displayed their finery. Balls and assemblies were held in the Stevens House as Lancaster's gentry waltzed under the glowing and hissing gas chandeliers.

During the post-Civil War Era, Republican party strength in the county developed rapidly. Except in the city, Columbia, and Marietta, Republican victories were complete at each election.

Between the Civil War and 1900 Lancaster's industry prospered in its diversity, but the business leaders were farsighted enough to realize new industries had to be brought in to replace those that would fall victim to technological progress.

The first generation of industry had ended with the Civil War and the second generation already showed subtle signs of decline, highlighted perhaps by the business depression of 1873. Business leaders met occasionally to discuss the future of Lancaster's economy. This concern led to the establishment of a board of trade in the 1870s.

By the end of the 19th century the efforts of the board of trade had begun to bear fruit. Its officers welcomed new industries but, much to their credit, they discouraged enterprise of dubious quality. A good credit rating, a reputation for quality production, and a sound, conservative stability were the

Some citizens ignored Victorian social restrictions and sported about in pleasure carriages, showing off their finery. This six-horse tallyho belonged to Eli B. Powl of 14-16 East Walnut Street in Lancaster.

Lancaster city showed contrasts in appearance as the Victorian Era came of age. The stores nearest Penn Square, which dated from the late 18th and early 19th centuries, were modernized by adding the latest Victorian facades. This 1885 view of the south side of East King Street shows the Victorian stores west of South Duke Street and much earlier stores beyond Duke Street at the left.

As advertised at the left, Lawrence Knapp's Empire Brewery supplied beer to Lancastrians. Lawrence Siegler, pictured at right, dispensed it in his saloon at 333 Church Street.

criteria by which prospective businesses were judged. Incoming industries were expected to exhibit acceptable business ethics.

A pair of Lancaster businessmen took the local tradition for ingenuity, resourcefulness, and technical perfection a step beyond what the board of trade had in mind. In the 1890s a leaf-tobacco dealer and the owner of a cigar factory began making and using counterfeit revenue stamps. The perfection of the engraving and quality of paper, complete with the USIRS watermark, all executed in the finest tradition of Lancaster craftsmen, enabled the enterprising partners to fool the federal agents.

Flushed with such success, they went into the production of paper money, applying the same skills in engraving and paper preparation. Again they were successful—until some clerk noticed the color of the seal was faded. The suspected bill was pronounced genuine by the Bureau of Engraving and Printing of the Treasury Department. The Secret Service was bothered, however, so the legendary detective William Burns was called in. Shortly after that it was found the "genuine" money was a Lancaster creation of Kendig and Jacobs. To this day the federal government claims the Lancaster-made bills to be the most perfect counterfeits ever discovered.

Despite the prosperity of the farms, the idyllic villages and rural beauties of Lancaster County, the city had grown smug, contented, and quite ugly. The streets were dirty, the wooden awnings over the sidewalks in front of downtown stores darkened the city. Immorality, prostitution, and drunkenness were all too evident. Out of this gradually rose a spirit of reform and progressiveness spearheaded by several enlightened merchants and

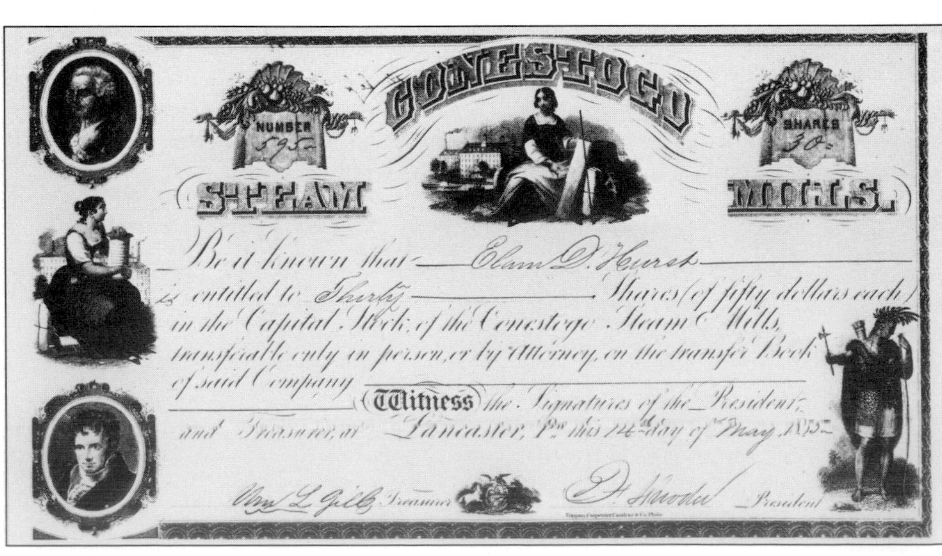

Lancaster's first large industry conducted at one site was the Conestoga Steam Cotton Mills, begun in 1847. The mills provided employment to hundreds of female operatives but few dividends to stockholders.

manufacturers.

Lancaster County looked forward to increased and sustained prosperity. Technological obsolescence was a nagging threat that bothered the more perceptive businessmen. Reliance on the cigar and carriagemaking industries was unwise. The anthracite iron industry with its blast furnaces and rolling mills no longer was a major factor in the local economy as newer plants in western Pennsylvania replaced them. Still, there remained the Lancaster work ethic that spelled the difference between success or failure in business.

As telephone service developed during the late 1880s, the streets of downtown Lancaster were darkened by hundreds of wires strung along clusters of cross-arms, each telephone having a wire. The Independent Telephone Company competed with the Bell Telephone Company in providing service. At one time the telephone exchange was on the top floor of Old City Hall, the wires to subscribers radiating out from an ugly boxlike tower sitting on the roof.

Daniel S. Bursk, wholesale and retail grocer, and grandfather of Lieutenant General Daniel Bursk Strickler, stands with his horse and delivery wagon on East King Street in 1891.

Watt and Shand, two Scottish dry goods merchants started their store in 1878, known as "The New York Store." They made a careful study of Lancastrians' needs and preferences in quality, then set about to fulfill them, probably little realizing that a century later their descendants would own the largest department store in Lancaster, growing with prosperity while others failed and closed their doors.

Leinbach and Company

Lancaster's cigar and tobacco industries flourished in the late 1800s, employing hundreds of workers at many factories and warehouses. Local businessman John Fendrich operated a cigar factory and sold tobacco products from his Gay Nineties shop at Front and Locust streets in Columbia.

Said to be the longest silk mill in the nation, the Stehli Silk Mill was built in the 1890s. Throwing and weaving of silk textiles was a major industry in Lancaster County in the early 20th century. Located northeast of the city, the building is now used as a warehouse.

opened "The Boston Store" on North Queen Street, suggesting New York may be brash and new, but Boston was the center of culture, learning, and traditional quality. Leinbach's store had a large, open court soaring up through five stories to skylights. Balconies enclosed the courtlike boxes in the opera house, while green shrubs, vines, and ferns grew around the edges.

On East King Street several large dry goods stores competed. Fahnnestock's later to be Garvin's, Williamson and Foster, and Hoar and McNabb attracted the folk that were suspicious of Boston and New York fashions. Hager and Brother continued to operate from the dingy little store begun in 1821, and would refuse to budge until the 20th century. For those talented ladies that made their own stylish clothing there was Astrich's Palace of Fashion at 115 North Queen Street for the latest ribbons, bows, feathers, and hats.

Lancaster's water supply continued to be the Conestoga River from which waterwheel-powered pumps sent raw water to the town's reservoirs located east of the prison between King and Orange streets. The ancient machinery, installed in 1837 when the original waterworks was constructed, no longer was capable of serving a city of 35,000 people, even when assisted with the steam pumps added in 1878. Lancaster was growing rapidly in the northeastern and northwestern portions, the most remote areas from the pumps and reservoirs.

Late in 1888 a new pumping station was built along the Conestoga River near the railroad bridge at the Grofftown Road. Two large steam pumps operated with a daily capacity of 11 million gallons. These were placed on a reserve basis in 1929 when eight electrically driven and three gasoline-powered pumps were installed. This plant was removed in 1976, having been replaced with a small pumping station in the 1950s, used to augment the city's water-treatment plant along the Susquehanna River in Columbia.

Lancaster's water was used untreated until 1907. A large reservoir built in Buchanan Park in the 1890s burst during the initial filling, flooding the west end. A small wading pool marks the site.

Of considerably greater interest to the water committees of

Major Industries in Lancaster County

Rank	1860	1870	1880
1	Flour milling	Flour milling	Flour milling
2	Pig iron	Pig iron	Iron (pig, wrought)
3	Wrought iron	Cotton textiles	Cotton textiles
4	Cotton textiles	Leather goods	Cigars
5	Leather goods	Wrought iron	Leather goods
6	Liquor, distilled	Cigars	Carriages, wagons
7	Agricultural implements	Carriages, wagons	Foundry, machine products
8	Leather boots, shoes	Clothing, men's	Hats, wool
9	Lumber, sawed	Lime	Clothing, men's
10	Carriages, wagons	Agricultural implements	Lumber, sawed
11	Iron ore	Woolen goods	Corks, bottle stoppers
12	Blacksmith products	Lumber, sawed	Beer, malt beverages
13	Lime	Beer, malt beverages	Furniture
14	Clothing, men's	Paper, printing	Agricultural implements
15	Beer, malt beverages	Machinery, steam engines	Printing, publishing
16	Iron castings	Tin, copper, sheet metal	Tin, copper, sheet metal
17	Furniture	Hats, wool	Paper (for printing)
18	Saddlery, harness	Furniture	Bread, bakery goods
19	Nickel ore, spelter	Bricks	Saddlery, harness
20	Tin, copper, sheet metal	Millwork (planing mill)	Millwork (planing mill)
21	Woolen goods	Iron castings	Bricks
22	Cigars	Coal oil, rectification	Watches
23	Paper (for printing)	Bread, bakery goods	Confectionery
24	Rifles	Saddlery, harness	Malt (for brewing)
25	Meat packing	Medicines, patent medicines	Meat packing

The diversity of Lancaster's business community is well illustrated by the producers of such lesser-known items as soap. In this 1905 view a load of naphtha soap is being shipped elsewhere by rail. Charles Miller's soap works was located on South Prince Street at Seymour Street.

The first automobile built in Lancaster was this handcrafted horseless carriage made at the Safety Buggy Works about 1903. The "assembly line" is in the blacksmith shop of the buggy factory then located near Rossmere. Later the Rowe Company built trucks in a factory on Fountain Avenue. Others built cars and trucks in small numbers from time to time without enduring success.

the city councils than planning for replacement and expansion of the water facilities was how the water was to be used. After Jacob Demuth put a bathtub in his home in 1839, one of the first bathtubs in the Republic, the city was aghast when eight more tubs appeared in city homes; and to make the well-washed citizens pay their proper share, each tub was assessed three dollars annually.

Most physicians in Lancaster were not convinced frequent bathing was healthy, but one doctor demonstrated the courage of his convictions by putting in his own tub in 1849. Dr. John Light Atlee, a leader in the healing arts, was the straw that broke the camel's back—the city charged him $30. Out came the tub. The city relented and lowered the annual charge for tubs to $16.

Until the germ theory was understood in the 1880s, health care and sanitation were not critical matters to Lancastrians. Cholera deaths in 1832 and 1854 were attributed to fogs and musty clods of putrefying organic matter decaying along the streams and canal.

In 1854 the borough of Columbia had 127 deaths in a cholera epidemic. Town officials frantically built smoky fires in the gutters, thinking the thick smoke would destroy the causes of the epidemic. One Lancastrian, however, believed differently. Dr. John L. Atlee, owner of the bathtub and one of the nation's most distinguished physicians, thought some organic substance he could see in his microscope probably was the cause of cholera. Dr. Koch proved him correct about 30 years later.

The medical practitioners in 19th-century Lancaster were among the most innovative and skilled physicians in the nation; they created a pioneering tradition that continues to bring laurels to their professional descendants. The Pennsylvania Medical Society was organized in Lancaster by local physicians in 1848; the local society having been founded in 1844. When he was 83 years old, Dr. John L. Atlee was elected president of the American Medical Association. His brother, Washington L. Atlee, was a pioneer in surgery, having perfected the safe removal of ovarian tumors.

When the Pennsylvania Medical Society refused to recognize

women as physicians, the Lancaster group urged the state unit to change its policy. Female physicians practiced in Lancaster without hostility from the local male population. Dr. Mary E. Wilson was practicing medicine as early as 1875 and Dr. Elizabeth Keding, who opened her office in 1886, was still treating patients at the age of 88.

The 20th century ushered in the automobile age. Milton S. Hershey announced that his candy factory would have the first motorcar in town in 1900; it was a Riker Electric Vehicle. By 1904 Samuel K. Landis was selling and repairing autos in a garage at 126 East Orange Street. He sold Reo, EMF 30, Premier, and Haynes motorcars. Three years later S. G. Roth established the National Auto Company, Inc., at Duke and Vine streets, which later was the home of the Conestoga Truck Company.

Lancaster had hopes of becoming the Detroit of the East when Samuel Rowe built his motor-vehicle factory in 1918, just in time to land—and lose—a contract for building army trucks. The plant went into receivership in 1925 and one of the surviving buildings was part of the DeWalt Division of the Black and Decker Company. Industries supplying the auto trade sprang up in Lancaster, chief among them the K-D Manufacturing Company.

World War I created ideological problems in many Lancaster families in which several generations of German immigrants lived. Few had much regard for Kaiser Wilhelm II, but their hearts sank at mention of "Krauts" and "bloodthirsty Huns." Emotions brought about the renaming of German Street to Farnum Street, and Freiburg Street to Pershing Avenue. Liberty bonds were sold in Penn Square (Old Centre Square) in a small version of the old courthouse that was in the square.

Lancaster industries produced for the war effort, Lancastrians observed meatless Mondays and heatless Tuesdays and the city's matrons rolled bandages for the Red Cross. Lancaster's young men and

Lancaster went all out to celebrate the 200th anniversary of the founding of Lancaster County in 1929. Here, a group of prominent young Lancastrians practice for the Pageant of Gratitude on the grounds of Franklin and Marshall College. Biesecker Gymnasium is visible in the background.

Cassius Emlen Urban was Lancaster's first native architect. He designed churches, hotels, commercial structures, and homes in the 1890s and continued practicing his profession until his retirement and death in the early 1930s. Among his larger structures are the Griest Building, the Reformed Theological Seminary, and buildings at Hershey.

women enlisted in the armed forces or waited for their draft notices from President Wilson. When the armistice was announced, Lancaster's factory whistles blew continuously for hours and the population went wild.

Sensing that Republican control of Lancaster city was threatened by progressive merchants and businessmen, William Walton Griest, the untitled GOP (Grand Old Party) political leader, ran highly respected men for mayor, a strategy that worked until 1922. In that year a coalition of progressive Democrats and independent Republicans were swept into office. During the following eight years the city was spruced up, wires went underground, and streets were reconstructed.

The board of trade eventually became the Lancaster Chamber of Commerce. The Lancaster Manufacturers Association represented the interests of local industry and encouraged the development of diversified manufacturing.

Despite its economic successes, the city continued to have major social problems caused by widespread drinking and prostitution. In 1914 a revitalized Law and Order Society under the leadership of the rector of St. James's Episcopal Church, Dr. Clifford G. Twombley, drew attention to the sordid conditions until the law enforcement agencies were forced into action. Within a few years the city was relatively free of vice and it has remained clean except for short periods during Prohibition and World War II.

Cassius Emlen Urban, Lancaster's own distinguished architect, was kept busy in the late 19th and early 20th centuries designing fine new buildings such as the Woolworth Building (1899), Hotel Brunswick (1914), Griest Building (1923), and numerous churches and residences. High schools for boys (1916) and girls (1904) replaced Victorian buildings. The Lancaster General Hospital commenced a building program in 1902. Banks erected fine new structures to correspond to their pre-Depression financial strength.

During the Roaring Twenties Lancaster's breweries were hit hard. Beer could not be brewed legally. Outside mobs moved into the city and operated one of the breweries and a number of stills. The Rieker Brewery transported its unlawful product through a hose line strung through the West King and North Water streets' sewers.

Police raids were infrequent and disobedience was rampant.

On parade—in June 1928, a unit of the 28th Division, Pennsylvania National Guard World War I was reviewed by citizens and accompanied by a marching band.

Lieutenant General Daniel Bursk Strickler is Lancaster County's highest ranking military officer. The much-decorated and honored officer was the youngest combat officer in World War I. During World War II, in the Battle of the Bulge, he was able to hold off the enemy for days and eventually extricated his troops from their perilous mission. He served as lieutenant governor of Pennsylvania from 1947 to 1950.

Finally the corruption and disregard for the law moved the city to take action. A police lieutenant was murdered by an outside mob for refusing to cooperate. Colonel Daniel Bursk Strickler, a much-decorated officer of World War I and a Lancaster attorney, was persuaded to assume temporary command of the police department. In less than a year Commissioner Strickler was able to return to his private life and profession after cleansing the police system. To the great credit of the city police, Colonel Strickler's work has remained an object of integrity that is followed faithfully.

Several major banks failed in the early 1930s and unemployment rose during the Depression of 1931–1935. Nevertheless, Lancaster County's economy was much healthier than other places in Pennsylvania, a condition brought about by its diversified economy and the reputation of its work force. No major manufacturers ceased operations. Government-aided relief programs provided needed municipal improvements such as sewers, water treatment facilities, street reconstruction, and school buildings.

When the guns started blazing in 1939, Americans were divided on the issue of remaining neutral or taking sides in the war then beginning in Europe. Lancastrians discussed the matter earnestly, but when Pearl Harbor was attacked they hastened to the armed forces recruiting offices to enlist. Local industries swung into war production, with Armstrong Cork Company making shells, airplane fuselages, bomb racks, camouflage netting, and other articles of warfare.

Hamilton Watch Company turned its heritage of precision timepiece production to making marine chronometers, air-force watches, and map-measuring tools. The U.S. Navy established a plant operated by RCA to make electronic devices, and this plant, now owned by Burle Industries, continues as one of Lancaster's major industries. A modernistic glass-and-wood structure was built in Penn Square to sell war bonds and stamps. J. P. McCaskey High School created a Victory Corps program in which most of the students participated, doing their part to win the war. Air-raid tests, civil-defense

Lancaster County's skilled machinists have manufactured weapons since the French and Indian wars. During World War II, Armstrong Cork Company (now Armstrong World Industries) produced millions of shells, aircraft fuselages, and a multitude of other wartime items. Some of the lathes that were used by Armstrong to make 20 mm shells are pictured here.

During the 1940 presidential campaign, Republican candidate Wendell Wilkie visited Lancaster to drum up support among the party faithful. He is pictured here in front of the Pennsylvania Railroad station (now Amtrak) with Lancaster's Congressman J. Roland Kinzer (far left) and Massachusetts Congressman Joseph Martin. Lancaster's Republican leadership displayed lukewarm support for Wilkie, and he carried the county only 44,913 votes to Roosevelt's 32,170.

wardens, and victory gardens became the order of the day.

Earl F. Rebman, a local merchant and candy manufacturer, was put in charge of gathering salvageable materials for the war effort, and he was so successful that other communities across the nation were urged to imitate Lancaster. Thousands of local citizens unable to serve in the armed forces served on numerous government boards, helping with rationing, housing, and civil defense. Lancaster's volunteerism tradition had its finest hour.

In 1942 Lancaster celebrated its 200th anniversary, but the clouds of war hung heavy and there was little festivity. The citizenry did take enough time out to help the

Young Lancastrians were caught up in the joy that swept the city as Germany surrendered in 1945. These carrier boys would see older brothers and fathers return home as soon as the war in the Pacific ended. (Lancaster New Era*)*

German prisoners of war found Lancaster a congenial place to work despite the ever-present guards. Those men captured in southern Germany found the Pennsylvania-German dialect fairly easy to understand. Here POWs are at work in a Lancaster tobacco warehouse. (Lancaster New Era)

Lancaster County Historical Society place a plaque in city hall, by now occupying the old federal building on North Duke Street.

At the end of the war, an immense victory parade was held June 14, 1946, giving Lancastrians a festive time to express their gratitude. Lancaster then turned its attention to conversion of wartime industries to peacetime production. Temporary unemployment resulted when all government contracts were canceled at once, but local businesses had planned for that eventuality and the distress did not last long.

Despite the perceived conservatism of its people and their attachment to practical matters, Lancaster has produced and supported many outstanding artists, musicians, and writers. The humanities have been nurtured for nearly two centuries in Lancaster; the 1879 Cliosophic Society, the Fortnightly Club, the Torch Club, and other societies devoted to discussing scholarly essays have been nourishing the Lancastrians for generations.

With its reputation as a conservative community, Lancaster might be thought of as a place not supportive of the equality of women. Such is not the case. Women from the times of Susannah Wright, Ann LeTort, and Marie Ferree, right down to the present have made their marks in Lancaster. They have been accepted as peers in the professions and business world. The 150-year old Lancaster City-County Medical Society championed the cause of female physicians from the beginning. In business, education, arts, and the social services, Lancaster women have proved their equality.

Municipal planning began in 1929 with the Nolan Comprehensive Plan for Lancaster, but Lancaster preferred to dream and dawdle until the Depression ended all notions of boulevards and parks along the Conestoga River and Little Conestoga Creek, and other ideas of making the ancient town into the City Beautiful. There were more practical concerns than galleries, libraries, museums, and handsome public buildings.

Toward New Horizons

A contemporary fountain enlivens Penn Square, a commercial hub for 250 years. (Mark E. Gibson)

Before victory was won in World War II, Lancaster was preparing for the future. In the decades between the wars, the city had grown rather seedy and much of the downtown property had become shabby. Many commercial structures were uninviting and slum housing covered much of the southeast area.

In 1945, Lancaster commissioned Michael Baker to prepare a comprehensive plan for the city. From the Baker Plan evolved codes for housing, zoning, and other regulations giving the city authority over correction of physical conditions. A city planning commission with a professional staff was appointed. Renewal of slum housing and deteriorating commercial properties was placed under the control of the Lancaster Redevelopment Authority. To preserve the more deserving buildings of architectural and historical merit, as well as to conserve the human setting of the city landscape, a historic district ordinance was enacted and a board of review was established to administer the policy.

Lancastrians are a highly individualistic people for whom planning, as a concept, smacked of government control. Civic improvement was not greeted with unanimous approval. Every step taken by the city government was roundly criticized by its opponents and just as vigorously praised from friendly quarters.

The mid-1950s saw much new construction in the city. In 1954 a new building was constructed for the Lancaster County Library, replacing an obsolete facility on the same site. During the same year a public safety building was erected at the northwest corner of Duke and Chestnut streets. The chaste structure with elements of contemporary and traditional style designed by its architect, H. C. Kreisle, houses the police and fire department headquarters. It was the first building constructed for the city government. The municipal building had been the Federal Building-Post Office from 1894 to 1932 and Old City Hall had been a hand-me-down from the county, 1854 to 1932.

Other major construction included Lancaster's three hospitals. Between 1952 and 1978 Lancaster General Hospital took form, replacing its half-century-old facilities and becoming in the process the largest single mass of structures in the city. The Victorian brick pile of St. Joseph Hospital was replaced by a vast new complex between 1950 and 1977. Lancaster Osteopathic Hospital, now known as the Community Hospital, in a series of building projects, constructed a large modern facility adjacent to the city in

Lancaster's notorious southeast quadrant contained most of the slum housing. Mayor George Coe, with paper in pocket, leads members of the Lancaster City Council and Redevelopment Authority on a tour of the area to be cleared in the 1960s.

Lancaster Township.

The center city was losing ground in its struggle to survive despite the efforts of Lancastrians to breathe new life into it. Eventually the city government concluded local property owners and businessmen either did not have faith in revitalization by private initiative or they lacked the means to grasp and solve the problem.

Lancastrians wanted something done, and done quickly, but it had to be accomplished within the structure and philosophy of Lancaster tradition. Outside entrepreneurs and followers of federal and state projects were suspect. The city administrations, one succeeding another, found themselves immobilized as urban renewal plodded along, leaving acres of cleared land strewn with broken bricks and sprouting wasteland weeds. It seemed as if Lancaster had lost its faith, imagination, and spirit.

In the early 1960s urban renewal was begun. Slum clearance started with removals of blocks of deteriorating housing, while public-

The country saloon provided opportunity to discuss politics, sports, the economy, and local affairs over generous portions of beer and liquor. This old-time bar at Ephrata's Mount Vernon Hotel still flourished in 1955. At far right is proprietor Frank Weinhold.

The Capitol Theatre boasted a handsome interior when it was built in the 1920s. Pictured here before its demolition in 1966, the west side of North Queen Street was once a busy district, then stood idle with weeds and rubble. Hamilton Bank and Armstrong World Industries constructed office buildings at the north and south ends of the block.

housing programs tried to provide homes for displaced residents. The worst slums were eliminated and salvageable structures were rehabilitated. Two blocks of downtown Lancaster including the YMCA, Hotel Brunswick, several smaller hotels, and four motion picture theaters were leveled. Eventually a new Hotel Brunswick and several large office buildings rose on the site. A new department store was built and lasted a short time before it became a factory producing defense items.

In the public's eyes, the gap between destruction and rebuilding was intolerably long. Complaints about destroying restorable structures were common. Within three years, however, much of the worst slum area, including the notorious Barney Google Row, was removed. Public housing developed such projects as Hickory Tree Heights in the southeast section near the Conestoga River.

The environmental and recreational concerns of the city were given public attention by the Conestoga Valley Association.

The east side of North Queen Street's second block was demolished in 1966 as part of an urban renewal project. A new hotel now stands on the site of the Hotel Brunswick but Lancastrians fondly remember the old Brunswick and its genial host, Paul Heine.

Former mayor Richard M. Scott poses with Tom Ratza, president of the Old Town Lancaster Corporation, which restored an area of 70 historical structures in the downtown area.

County Park and the restoration of General Edward Hand's historic 1784-era plantation, *Rock Ford*, are the result of efforts by enlightened county commissioners during the 1960s and 1970s. *Rock Ford* and its outbuildings have been preserved by the Junior League of Lancaster and a nonprofit foundation of the league. In the late 1930s President James Buchanan's mansion, *Wheatland*, was acquired and has been maintained as a museum under similar auspices. Both country homes are situated on beautifully landscaped grounds. They are fully furnished with elegant period pieces and are open to the public.

In April 1966 the city adopted a charter that replaced the commission form of government with a strong mayor-council scheme. The mayor would be a full-time executive and the council would be a legislative body.

The election of 1973 swept Richard M. Scott, a former Air Force brigadier general and onetime fighter pilot, into office on the Republican ticket. Voters had grown impatient with the empty spaces and bureaucratic inaction. Mayor Scott enlisted a number of community leaders and business interests in solving Lancaster's problems.

This approach was not new. But a new dimension emerged. With all the planning and demolishing and publicly funded programs there had been a missing ingredient: humanity. The mayor announced there would be a halt to tearing things down until there was something worthwhile as a replacement. The emphasis was put on rehabilitation, conservation, and on doing what citizens, rather than bureaucrats, wanted accomplished. The results were stunning.

The empty spaces filled up with the large new Hamilton Bank's regional headquarters and the immense design center and office building of the Armstrong Cork Company. The Hilton Inn became the Brunswick Hotel, reviving an honored name, warm memories, and, it was hoped, profitable operations. Plans were announced for the creation of shops between the hotel and the former department store building.

The center city was turned into a place of great beauty, with Penn Square and adjacent streets made both modern and traditional, and above all, a place for people rather than for motorcars and impersonal contrivances. While owners of commercial structures were urged to retain the worthwhile "old" aspects of their buildings, conformity to one age or style was out.

Meantime, residential neighborhoods throughout the city were spruced up partially through a publicly funded cooperative program (Neighborhood Improvement Program) and through private initiative of the property owners. John A. Jarvis spearheaded the program to encourage residents to bring out the beauty of their neighborhoods by their own efforts and thus generate much pride. This development has been extremely successful in converting block after block of dingy homes into neighborhoods of great charm and awakened pride.

In 1977 a seven-story annex for the courthouse was completed at the southwest corner of Duke and Orange streets.

During the 1960s the old Fulton Opera House, the queen of Prince Street at one time, now shabby and disreputable, was acquired by

When it was first built in 1854, the Lancaster County Courthouse served a population of about 100,000. In the last century and a half, it has undergone many renovations and additions to meet the current needs of more than 420,000 residents. (Mark E. Gibson)

Armstrong World Industries employs 23,500 people worldwide. Corporate headquarters and a manufacturing facility are located in Lancaster. (Dick Wanner)

the Fulton Opera House Foundation and restored lovingly to its early elegance. The house has been returned to its cultural function and is the home of the Lancaster Symphony Orchestra, one of the finest symphonic bodies to be found in the nation's smaller cities. Celebrating its 30th anniversary in 1977, the Lancaster Symphony attracts as its guest musicians the leading artists of the nation.

Music always has been a significant part of the Lancaster heritage, stemming from the emphasis placed by the Lutheran, Moravian, and Reformed churches . Pro Musica Sacra, a choral and instrumental group directed by Dr. Carl Schroeder, performs sacred music of the Baroque period.

The Lancaster Opera Company has earned a reputation well beyond Lancaster for the professional quality of its performances. Although the bands so prevalent in the 1870 to 1915 period have disappeared, the Malta Band has continued to provide music for the city's ceremonies and performs with rare musicianship. The Musical Arts Society and its junior group play important roles in the serious musical life of the community.

Art also is a major ingredient in Lancaster heritage. From the days in the early 19th century when Jacob Eichholtz and Arthur Armstrong painted portraits of prominent citizens, to Charles Demuth in the 20th century, the visual arts have been celebrated in Lancaster. The Lancaster County Art Association, after a period of activity in the 1930s, was reorganized in 1948 and its many activities continue to serve the artistic community. Other art groups, some oriented more to the abstract or nonrepresentative modes of visual art, flourish in Lancaster. The arrival of spring always brings art shows to the sidewalks of downtown.

The Lancaster County Historical Society, founded in 1886 as a successor to the Historical, Agricultural, and Mechanics' Society of 1857, occupied its new fireproof building adjacent to *Wheatland* in 1956. Recognized throughout North America and Europe for the quality of its research, publications, and holdings, the society attracts scholars and historians to its library and archives.

Incorporated in 1971, the Heritage Center of Lancaster County acquired the Old City Hall and Masonic lodge buildings from the city and, with the support of the county commissioners and the James Hale Steinman Foundation, converted the structures to an unusually high-quality museum of Lancaster's finest creations in the arts and crafts. The late 19th-century buildings

Steinman Park in downtown Lancaster is the perfect spot for lunch breaks—a half block from the Square. (Dick Wanner)

Downtown Lancaster at noon brings out shoppers, tourists, and business professionals—for walking, browsing, or a bite to eat. (Dick Wanner)

have been restored in exterior appearance and this work will continue in years to come. The North Museum of Franklin and Marshall College operates in a new building, and is an outstanding natural history museum and planetarium.

Human rights issues were examined with renewed interest. Public swimming pools did not exist in the 1950s, and privately owned swimming pools had the custom of not admitting black persons. Civil rights groups protested and held demonstrations. Lancaster city and county then built large public pools that are open to everyone. The war in Vietnam prompted many marches and demonstrations by students and religious pacifists. Other demonstrations took place, all of them relatively peaceful, and Lancastrians learned to live with a changing society, as had their ancestors.

Lancaster County's leaders have recognized that future economic success depends on an educated citizenry. In addition to Franklin and Marshall College, Millersville University, and Elizabethtown College, the county's institutions of higher education include the Lancaster Bible College, chartered in 1972. This Christian and Bible-centered school is an outgrowth of the Lancaster School of the Bible founded in 1933 by the Reverend Henry J. Heydt. The degree-granting college occupies a 36-acre campus northeast of the city.

Lancaster also hosts branch campuses for the Pennsylvania State University, Lebanon Valley College, Millersville University, and Harrisburg Area Community College. Studies are being conducted to determine a need for a Lancaster County Community College. Located in downtown Lancaster on North Prince Street, the Pennsylvania School of Art and Design offers classes in the visual arts including commercial art, graphics, photography, and design—product, industrial, and fashion. The Lancaster General Hospital and St. Joseph Hospital operate fine schools of nursing in cooperation with Millersville University.

The Thaddeus Stevens State School of Technology, formerly the Thaddeus Stevens Trade School, established in 1905, partially by a bequest from the "Old Commoner,"

Homemade ice cream is the specialty at the Strasburg Country Store and Creamery. (Mark E. Gibson)

Top: Since 1889, the striking Strasburg Train Station has been a community landmark. (Audrey Gibson)

Center: A typical tavern is just one of the displays at the Landis Valley Museum in Lancaster, a scenic hamlet of more than 15 historic buildings. (Mark E. Gibson)

Bottom: Blacksmithing is demonstrated at Mill Bridge Village, which also has a 1738 operating grist mill. (Mark E. Gibson)

Top: Amish farmers are not permitted by their religion to use self-propelled vehicles or farm machinery. Here, horses pull contemporary farm equipment. (Mark E. Gibson)

Center: American crafts traditions such as these handmade quilts are an integral part of life in Lancaster County. (Mark E. Gibson)

Bottom: Lancaster County boasts highly productive farmland and the best non-irrigated agricultural land in the nation. A well-maintained farm complex stands next to harvested fields, awaiting winter. (Dick Wanner)

Top: Long's Park playground in Lancaster, was constructed entirely with donated materials and volunteer labor. (Dick Wanner)

Bottom: The congregation of Trinity Lutheran Church is Lancaster's oldest. Begun in 1761, the church was completed in 1794, when its steeple was installed. The handsome Georgian tower contains a full chime of bells and is decorated with statues of the four evangelists. (Dick Wanner)

has been educating young men—and now women—in the construction, mechanical, and electronic skills necessary for success in today's competitive economy. The state-owned school occupies a well-equipped campus along East King Street near South Broad Street.

During the 1970s and 1980s economic changes rapidly occurred in Lancaster County. Shopping centers and malls built on the outskirts of Lancaster city and most boroughs and towns removed the retail traffic from old business districts. Stores established for many generations closed. Downtown merchants struggled to hold on to their trade. Studies were made to discover ways for keeping the traditional shopping areas alive. Various promotional events, efforts to rehabilitate aging buildings and to spruce up dingy streets, and increased police patrols to make the older neighborhoods safe for shoppers were tried. Despite the heroic efforts to revitalize downtown shopping centers the lack of free parking and fears of being attacked or robbed continued to thwart positive results.

In 1991 downtown Lancas-

Top: Neff's Mill Covered Bridge spans the Pequea Creek between West Lampeter and Strasburg townships. It was first built in 1824 by Christian Brackbill and was 103 feet long. In 1875, the bridge was rebuilt by James C. Carpenter at a cost of about $1,800. (Courtesy, John H. Ramsay, Jr.)

Bottom: Field hockey is a winner, in a match between Millersville University and Franklin and Marshall College. (Dick Wanner)

ter business leaders organized DID (Downtown Investment District) for the purpose of revitalizing that area. The efforts to make the shopping district cleaner, safer, and more attractive were to be financed by a modes assessment of those properties in the district, but strong resistance was mounted by those opposed to paying the fee.

Other communities in the county have tried, with some success, to make their traditional shopping centers more attractive. The overbuilding of shopping malls in the 1980s has contributed to the competition. Park City Mall, a huge complex with four major department stores and over 100 smaller stores, located at the crossing of the Harrisburg Pike and Route 30, has free parking for many thousands of automobiles. Frequent bus service brings city shoppers, especially the elderly, to the mall. Air conditioned in the summer and heated in the cold months, the mall is a comfortable place to shop and to be part of the crowd.

Economic dislocations occurred in Lancaster County dur-

WATT & SHAND

ing the 1980s as leveraged buy-outs and mergers removed local control, and occasionally closed long-established corporations. Family-owned businesses passed into hands of strangers whose motives, thought Lancaster Countians, surely were not sympathetic with the local ethic. Unemployment of executives and managers along with other employees caused chills in the economy. In some instances the purchasers of local businesses infused much needed capital and created a wider market; in other cases the result was plant closure and unemployment. Whatever the result, the economic disorganization was nerve-shattering to many Lancastrians. The recessions of the 1980s and 1990s aggravated the uneasiness.

Yet, Lancaster County's economy has remained the healthiest in Pennsylvania, employment is high, and Lancaster County schools continue to graduate students whose academic accomplishments have enabled them to enter the most demanding colleges and universities.

Although experiencing challenges of modern society, Lancaster County remains a place of exceptional beauty, of pastoral scenes and tranquil villages, of diverse peoples living in relative harmony. Change is gradual and is accepted only after experience and deliberation pronounce it worthwhile and necessary.

In recent years, as pristine farmland has been converted to housing developments and shopping centers, the survival of that unique quality of life so much admired is questioned. Fortunately, the county government and its planning commission have demonstrated a determination to see that reasonable change need not ruin the best that characterizes Lancaster County. Inherent in that distinctive life-style is an enterprising enthusiasm that maintains a balance between the material and the spiritual.

Despite the many physical changes to Lancaster's appearance over the years—the disappearance of the beloved old buildings and the construction of fresh, new structures boldly displaying an unfamiliar architecture—the community has never looked better. It bursts with pride, and for good reason. It is a handsome city.

The heritage of Lancaster is everywhere. Architectural geegaws pop up at every turn, delighting visitors and amazing longtime residents who never before took a close look. The old William Bausman Building at 121 East King Street sports an impish face that belongs to an eavesdropper, a face that probably amused Lancaster's barristers a decade before the American Revolution. Symbols are worked into the frieze of the Griest Building and faces of Neptune glare down from the facade of the venerable Lincoln Hotel. Animals abound in terracotta ornamentation throughout the city. Lions guard the professional offices at 126 East Chestnut Street and marvelous horned creatures embellish the facade of the Southern Market.

Lancaster does not have a distinctive architectural style. It is not known for a single institution that is unique and it has no one citizen in its history who stands above all others. Diversity, reasonable tolerance, compassion tempered with common sense, pragmatism, and independence are traits that characterize Lancastrians.

H. L. Mencken loved to visit Lancaster County, and probably had that in mind when he wrote (from H. L. Mencken, *Prejudices: Fifth Series,* 1926, p.11):

"Its essence lies in its permanence, in its capacity for accretion and solidification, in its quality of representing, in all its details, the personalities of the people who live in it."

Penn Square, at the center of Lancaster, is marked by the Soldiers and Sailors Monument dedicated July 4, 1984 to the memory of Lancaster Countians who have given their lives in the service of the Republic. Granite figures of a sailor, cavalryman, infantryman, and artilleryman stand guard around the plinth, which is surmounted by the Genius of Liberty. The site was the location of the first two courthouses and the place where the Continental Congress was held September 17, 1777. (Dick Wanner)

Partners in Progress

Excellent facilities for manufacturing, service, and retail industries support Lancaster County's thriving business climate. (David Hollinger)

From the time of enterprising Native American traders to the peak of the Industrial Age on through to today's diverse industries, Lancaster County has reaped the benefits of abundant natural resources and industrious people.

Since colonial days, Lancaster's leaders encouraged skilled professionals to settle in their thriving community. They welcomed artisans, merchants, educators, and professionals who emigrated from all parts of the world and they carefully built a reputation for quality production, stability, and sound business practices.

These immigrants brought with them family traditions from their old countries, and, sparked by American qualities of hard work and individual enterprise, created a cultural center of extraordinary activity.

Powered by water, Lancaster County was filled with mills that processed flour, cotton, clover, oil, paper, lumber, silk, lace, and textiles. Ready access to iron ore and wood for charcoal led to a burgeoning industry of furnaces and foundries. Shops making shoes, tinware, furniture, barrels, wagons, and carriages evolved into production-line manufacturing facilities turning out everything from umbrellas, cigars, and watches to chocolate and electronics. With manufacturing came service professions in the arts, sciences, law, medicine, commercial development, and finance.

Early immigrants also established a variety of churches, educational institutions, and community-service organizations that have continued to this day. Along with a sincere interest in preserving a high quality of life, they are what makes life in Lancaster so pleasant.

Known for a long tradition of harmony and tolerance, Lancaster County is a special place to work and live. The county's unique system of values preserves the old ways of the Amish population while inventing the technology of the future.

Today's Lancaster County is reflective of trends across the country—from historic preservation, to assuring streets are safe, to meeting the challenges of worldwide markets. Yet, even as business and civic leaders plan and develop, Lancastrians travel the roads and use the buildings created centuries ago by people with foresight and vision.

The following pages tell the ongoing success stories of businesses and enterprises whose triumphs are reflective of the people. By sponsoring this publication, these organizations demonstrate the same motivating spirit and commitment to progress that have become the hallmark of Lancaster County and the legacy for generations to come.

The Lancaster Chamber of Commerce and Industry

The Southern Market Center, at 100 S. Queen Street, houses the offices of The Lancaster Chamber of Commerce and Industry.

It was likely one of the hottest days of the summer when a small group of Lancaster businessmen met in a second-floor room at 19 East King Street on July 22, 1872. But it was not the weather they met to discuss, nor did the summer heat detract from their purpose.

Outside their downtown meeting room, streets of cobblestone and dirt churned thick with mud each time it rained. Would not the commerce of the city be improved for all, they asked one another, if only the streets could be paved with a hard material that would allow water to run off?

Among the group, there was concern too that the public supply of water might not be sufficient as the city grew. Serious questions were also raised about the varied practices being followed in the granting of credit, and how beneficial it would be for everyone if in the area of credit the city's merchants and bankers would work more closely together.

Of course it was always useful to discuss the need for better transportation facilities, especially additional railroad lines. Then there were schools and public buildings to be constructed, and if the city was to gain its fair share of a growing economy, it most definitely would need a proper hotel in the middle of town.

It was not casual conversation that brought these business leaders together that day, but the seemingly endless concerns generated by a city bursting with life and potential.

So it was on that summer day in 1872 that Lancaster's Board of Trade was organized. The stated purpose of the group at that time was to "unite efforts to meet and solve business and specific problems of the day." By early spring of the following year, membership in the young organization already numbered "100 of the businessmen of the city," according to minutes from the meeting of March 1873.

At the time about 40 similar organizations had been formed in the United States, and the name "Chamber of Commerce" had already been adopted by some of them.

The Board of Trade and the Lancaster Retail Merchants' Association had common concerns for the city at the turn of the century, and in 1910 the two organizations consolidated to form The Lancaster Chamber of Commerce. Two years later another business organization that would eventually come under the Chamber's umbrella was chartered, the Lancaster Manufacturers' Association.

By this time the streets of Lancaster were being shared by an odd mixture of slow-moving, horse-drawn vehicles and the faster but far noisier newcomer, the automobile. It was all too clear to anyone with an eye to the future that the automobile would soon force even more changes on a city that, like a healthy child, always seemed to be outgrowing its newest clothing.

The need to pave streets occupied much of the Chamber's

efforts in the years between World War I and the Great Depression. Attention was also being paid to the equalization of property assessment, extending city limits, and ending the collection of tolls on the major roads leading into town—something almost every other city had already done.

A vote on property assessment in 1923 recorded the votes of 418 members of the Chamber.

Housing became an issue that involved the resources of the Chamber as the Depression continued to take its toll on local residents during the 1930s. During this time the Chamber formed joint committees with the city government to deal with the very practical problems of zoning, housing, sewers, and water lines.

Even local concern for winning World War II was evident in Chamber activities. A February dinner meeting in 1939 included a guest lecturer speaking on the topic, "What Will Stop Hitler?" Less than a month later, a joint committee of the Chamber and the Manufacturers' Association was formed to solicit more defense work for the Lancaster area.

Even before the war ended, the Chamber stated its desire to cooperate fully with both the city and the county to assure the prosperity of the entire community during the post-war period. The Chamber's post-war plan included employment, housing, sanitary facilities, fire and police protection, economic development, a cannery for farm products, schools, libraries, parks, zoning and building codes, and traffic controls.

By the mid-1970s the Chamber and the Manufacturers' Association were both located in the same building and were sharing common interests. To no one's surprise they joined forces in January 1977, becoming The Lancaster Chamber of Commerce and Industry (LCCI), the name retained by the organization to this day.

The present-day chamber is one of the largest in Pennsylvania, with 2,000 members and an annual budget of $1.5 million. It is accredited by the Chamber of Commerce of the United States, where it ranks among the top chambers in the country based on both its size and the scope of activities in which it is involved.

Among the affiliates started by the LCCI are the Economic Development Company in 1969; the Lancaster County Private Industry Council in 1980; Leadership Lancaster and Lancaster Enterprise, Inc., both formed in 1983; the Lancaster BizPAC in 1984; the Lancaster County Business Group on Health in 1984; and the EDC Finance Corporation in 1987.

Daniel C. Witmer, president of The Lancaster Chamber of Commerce and Industry.

The 16th Annual Banquet of the Lancaster Manufacturers' Association, held at the Hotel Brunswick, January 24, 1928.

Lancaster County Historical Society

The Lancaster County Historical Society is located at 230 North President Avenue, in the Willson Memorial Building.

Kept at the Willson Memorial Building are the records and minutes of the Lancaster County Chapter, Pennsylvania Society of Sons of the Revolution.

The Lancaster County Historical Society was established in 1886, a remainder of the Historical Agricultural and Mechanics Society, which began in 1857. The society originally met monthly to hear and discuss research papers presented by community scholars. Because two of the board members were also editors of the two major daily newspapers, all of the research papers were subsequently published. Ninety-five volumes of the *JOURNAL* of the Lancaster County Historical society have been printed to date.

Scholars from nearby Franklin and Marshall College, Millersville University, and the Theological Seminary of the German Reformed Church established the foundation and primary purpose of the historical society, from which it has not deviated in 107 years. The society's primary function has always been educational.

In 1901 the society was incorporated. It acquired its first home in 1924, but the brick and timber building had limited storage capabilities. Documents and manuscripts had to be stored out of the area in fire-resistant libraries—an inconvenience to researchers. As a result, an effort to bring all of the materials under one roof was spearheaded by the society under the leadership of Dr. George L. Heiges. Financed wholly by bequests of George B. Willson and his cousin, Mary Rettew, a brick, concrete, and steel building was erected in 1956 on a large tract adjacent to Wheatland, the preserved home of President James Buchanan. Known as the Willson Memorial Building, the home of the Lancaster County Historical Society is surrounded by the Louise Arnold Tanger Arboretum.

The site houses the Genealogical and Historical Research Library, which serves everyone from students to professional researchers. The archives of the Lancaster County Historical Society include an eclectic mix of personal papers and public documents. A large corps of volunteers works continuously in this area to improve access to these sources of primary data. The library is visited each year by more than 6,000 researchers from across the nation, who use its resources for family and scholarly research.

In addition to its vast genealogical holdings, the library and archives house more than 20,000 volumes, 380 cubic feet of records and manuscript materials, early county court and government records, tax assessment records from 1729 to 1940, and bound volumes of Lancaster newspapers from 1787 to 1936, with more recent issues on microfilm. The Jasper Yeates Law Library, containing 1,043 volumes of sixteenth-, seventeenth-, and eighteenth-century law books and reports, is also located in the library.

The society's Willson Memorial Building is host to other fine historical organizations: The Lancaster County Chapter, Pennsylvania Society of Sons of the Revolution—the only chapter in Pennsylvania; Grave Concern—a group of citizens interested in the preservation of historic graves and grave sites in Lancaster County; Friends of the Tanger Arboretum—members interested in preserving the arboretum surrounding the Willson Building; General George H. Thomas Camp 19, Sons of Union Veterans of the Civil War—legal descendant of the Grand Army of the Republic; Union Fire Company Number 1—the oldest fire company in continuing existence in the nation; and the General Society of the War of 1812—documented descendants from 1812 veterans. The society also sponsors the annual Lancaster County Civil War Encampment to honor Lancaster County's participation in the Civil War and provide an educational program for local schools.

In addition to fostering educational publications, the society has an extensive collection of local relics and artifacts. Among the exhibits featured, one will find remarkable collections of furniture, textiles, glass, ceramics, metals, musical instruments, and other artifacts of historical Lancaster County. The apparel and textile collections from eighteenth- through twentieth-century Lancaster County will soon be on display. Volunteers and professional staff are indexing them now and adding them to exhibits.

Prized for their artistic skill, genealogical value, and historical merit, more than 60 portraits of self-trained artist Jacob Eichholtz are owned by the Lancaster County Historical Society and are on view in the Library Reading Room.

More than 10,000 images of early twentieth-century Lancaster County have been printed from negatives retained at Darmstaetter's Store.

The grounds of the Willson Memorial Building—the Louise Arnold Tanger Arboretum—display more than 100 specimens. The Friends of the Tanger Arboretum are developing long-range plans for the grounds, as well as conducting tours and educational programs for members and guests.

Without losing its commitment to quality leadership, the society has evolved from a group of conservators to an association in which membership and activity is extended to every age, educational level, and position in life. Members make a significant contribution to the identification, preservation, and interpretation of the rich and varied history of Lancaster County.

Benefits of membership in the society are many. Among them are unlimited use of the research library; discounts on purchases at the Society Bookstore; training programs and tours to historical sites and research facilities; subscription to the *JOURNAL* and the bimonthly newsletter; and free publishing of genealogical queries in the society newsletter.

The society sponsors the annual Lancaster County Civil War Encampment.

The Historic Clothing and Textiles Collection—covering 18th- to 20th-century Lancaster County—will soon be on display.

Lancaster Malleable Castings Co.

Lancaster Malleable Castings Company's plant on Manheim Pike casts parts for leading manufacturers of mining, construction, trucking, farm, hardware, and electrical equipment.

Lancaster was the fourth-largest manufacturing city in Pennsylvania in 1910. Watch companies, silk mills, automobile factories, and iron and steel mills were some of the industries that boosted Lancaster to this position. A newcomer to the industrial mix that year was Lancaster Malleable Castings Company, which began operations in 1910 as the Lancaster Foundry Company. It manufactured grey iron castings, padlocks, and harness hardware.

In 1916 the company began producing malleable iron castings—which are not as brittle as grey iron castings—using a hand-fired melting furnace. Eventually, its entire production became dedicated to malleable iron products.

The company currently casts parts for leading manufacturers of mining, construction, trucking, farm, hardware, and electrical equipment throughout the eastern United States.

One of the founders of the company was Aaron B. Hess. In 1913, at the age of 18, his son, H. Lloyd Hess, became associated with the company and later took over its management. Lloyd was joined in 1933 by his brother, Aaron E. Hess, and in 1956 by his son, J. Robert Hess, who is the present general manager.

Lancaster Malleable operates a complete pattern-making and repair facility and performs machining and finishing operations on many of the castings it produces.

The company employs 325 workers, making it Lancaster County's 60th-largest employer. It also owns Stumpf Field, former home of the Lancaster Red Roses professional baseball team. The field is now made available for recreational sports and civic activities in conjunction with the Conestoga Sertoma Club.

J. Walter Miller Company

The J. Walter Miller Company, which produces precision castings in nonferrous metals for industry, remains a family business after more than a century of operation in Lancaster. Milton K. Morgan III became the fourth generation to enter the management of the company when he joined his father, Milton K. Morgan, Jr., at the East Chestnut Street plant in 1980. Milton K. Morgan, Sr., went to work for his father-in-law in 1941. J. Walter Miller started it all in 1887.

J. Walter Miller came to Lancaster from Chambersburg after the Civil War because the family's business there, a commercial nursery, had been burned during the Battle of Gettysburg. He started an electroplating business in a shop next to the Brunswick Hotel in 1887. It was one of the first businesses of its kind in the area.

He soon became one of a half-dozen designers and manufacturers of padlocks in Lancaster. A turn-of-the-century illustrated catalog advertised the company's variety of brass-plated hardware specialties in addition to the bronze and brass padlocks bearing the J.W.M. initials.

In 1907 Miller moved his business to the 400 block of East Chestnut Street. He built a music studio next to the company's main office building, and here his daughter taught music and gave recitals during the 1920s and 1930s.

Foundry work had been a sideline of the company for many years. But after World War II, J. Walter Miller and Milton K. Morgan, Sr., realized that there were better opportunities in this area than in electroplating or padlocks, so they began specializing in producing precision castings from copper-based alloys and aluminum. This part of the business grew, and now the J. Walter Miller Company is both a major manufacturer of sprinkler heads for fire protection systems and producer of commercial castings such as fittings, valves, and impellers. The company also produces a few specialty items like brass banks and brass quoits, the latter being the choice of dedicated quoit players.

The J. Walter Miller Company has been doing business for more than a century in Lancaster, producing precision castings in nonferrous metals for industry.

There are 80 employees in the 50,000-square-foot foundry, which contains the best environmental protection devices for its electric melting furnaces. "We've always been quality oriented," says Milton Morgan, Jr., "and that includes the air quality around our plant."

The company has other state-of-the-art equipment that enhances its production capabilities. Sand testing equipment and automated sand mulling and distribution equipment ensure top quality in this important component of close-tolerance sand castings. Squeezer molding equipment provides greater accuracy and finer craftsmanship in medium- and high-volume castings. Automatic core making eliminates human error in core preparation, while significantly increasing production speed.

The principle that has guided the J. Walter Miller Company during over a century of prosperous operation is giving the customer the best quality product, on time and at a competitive price. The key to meeting these goals rests with the employees. "A small business like ours will exist and thrive only as long as we have good people working for us," says Milton Morgan, Jr. "We have many long-time employees in the foundry whose experience is the backbone of our company."

Raub Supply Company

Joseph C. Schick, president and chief executive officer of Raub Supply Company.

The turn of the century was a boom time for Lancaster. Like the rest of the nation, the city was enjoying the economic upswing that followed the Spanish-American War. Among the dozens of companies that flourished in the Red Rose City at the time was the Lancaster Sheet Metal Company, now known as Raub Supply Company. Raub Supply is one of the top 29 wholesalers of plumbing, heating, and cooling supplies in the United States. In addition to these product lines, the company also distributes electrical supplies, pipe, valves, fittings, and industrial mill supplies.

The origin of Raub Supply Company goes back to a partnership formed in 1896 between Harry L. Raub, Edward Reilly, and Amos K. Raub for the purpose of doing sheet metal installation for Reilly Brothers and Raub, a Lancaster wholesale and retail hardware company. The installation business incorporated in 1898 as the Lancaster Sheet Metal Company, with Harry L. Raub as its first president. Over the years, other sheet metal installers came to the company for their supplies.

The company added plumbing and heating supplies to its stock, and in 1909 dropped the sheet metal installation business in order to concentrate on wholesaling. Ten years later, the growing company opened its first branch in Harrisburg. At the same time, the name was changed to Raub Supply Company.

Originally located at Marion and Christian streets, the Lancaster branch and corporate headquarters moved to their present location at the corner of James and Mulberry in 1923. Other branches were opened through the years, and Raub Supply now serves a seven-state area ranging from New York to Virginia.

Acquisitions also have played an important role in the expansion of the company. The first was in 1959, when Raub Supply purchased a branch of Case Elderfield Company in Olean, New York. Other acquisitions included the Careva Company in York, Pennsylvania, Fredericksburg Pipe and Supply Company in Fredericksburg, Virginia, and Lehigh Valley Plumbing Supply in Allentown, Pennsylvania. As the locations of these acquisitions indicate, Raub Supply decided to concentrate its business in geographically contiguous areas. It also decided to concentrate on its primary products—plumbing, heating, cooling, and electrical supplies, and industrial products—and sold its ancillary product and service lines of appliances and floor coverings.

Inventory and shipping are important to any wholesale business, and Raub Supply has built its business by ensuring that appropriate inventory is on hand, customer delivery is timely, and pricing is routinely competitive. The company achieved these objectives by being one of the first in the industry to computerize its purchasing department. A punch-card system, forerunner of today's electronic comput-

General offices and salesroom of Raub Supply Company, at Christian and Marion streets, Lancaster.

ers, served the company from 1954 until 1965. An IBM 1440 computer was installed in that year, and Raub Supply has kept up with advances in data processing technology ever since. Today the 11 branches located in Pennsylvania, New York, and Virginia are on-line with a system that provides instant access to order entry, purchasing, receiving, and accounts payable.

The Raub family sold the business in 1976 to D.L. Wallace and C.A. Packard. In 1986 the company was purchased by Joseph C. Schick, who is currently chairman, president, and chief executive officer. "We at Raub Supply Company will be celebrating our first century as an incorporated business in Lancaster in 1998," Schick says. "So as you can see, we have been a significant part of Lancaster's history. In fact, we like to think that we may have supplied a majority of the vital plumbing, heating, and electrical components making up the internal infrastructures that have supported this city through the years. In keeping with local values and traditions, Raub Supply Company started as a family-owned business in 1896 and is today still a family-owned business, carrying on the tradition of its founder, Amos Raub, to supply quality products at a fair price to our customers."

Alumax Mill Products

The original Alumax Building.

With a major world war behind them, Americans in greater numbers than ever went back to work in 1946, touching off the greatest period of manufacturing growth the nation had ever seen. A part of this growth in Lancaster began almost unnoticed that year in a small, abandoned railroad freight station in Leola. Here the first five employees of the New Holland Metals Company set about making corrugated aluminum sheet to be used as roofing and siding on farm and industrial buildings. The enterprise was a venture of the New Holland Machine Company, a growing firm already busy at the time making a highly successful hay baler.

The freight station soon proved too small, and the operation was moved to Mountville in 1948. There, additional equipment was added to the original sheet corrugator, and the young company, with 15 employees, added rain-carrying systems to its aluminum products line.

New Holland Metals had grown to 100 employees by 1950, when it was separated from its parent company. With the financial support of Raymond Buckwalter, who also had an interest in the New Holland Machine Company, it was renamed Quaker State Metals Company and moved into a new plant on the Buckwalter farm. The farm, located along the Manheim Pike in what was then suburban Lancaster, is the present site of Alumax Aluminum.

The firm was purchased by Karl F. Leiberknect, Inc., a Reading machinery manufacturer, in 1958, and quickly thereafter was sold to Haille Mines. When Haille Mines merged with the Howe Sound Corporation, Quaker State assumed its new owner's name and, now with 225 employees, added a hot mill, additional cold mills, and finishing equipment to its Route 72 plant.

In 1962, the Paris-based firm of Pechiney Ugine Kuhlmann, a metals, chemicals, and nuclear

The Alumax plant in Lancaster.

energy company, acquired controlling interest in Howe Sound Corporation and by 1965 had eliminated any confusion in the company name by changing it to the Howmet Corporation.

By now the product line included not only rolled aluminum and rain-carrying systems, but also soffit, fascia, skylights, shutters, and other building products. The Manheim Pike operations were separated into two divisions in 1968, with the Building Products Division, known today as Alumax Home Products, moving to the Hempfield Industrial Park, and the Mill Products Division remaining at the Manheim Pike location.

Pechiney Ugine Kuhlmann gained complete control of the company in 1975 and changed the name to Howmet Aluminum Corporation. The firm then became part of the growing international family of Alumax, Inc., in 1983.

Today, Alumax Mill Products occupies 87 acres on the original Manheim Pike site and has a manufacturing capacity of over 300 million pounds of aluminum products a year. Products made in the plant, such as rigid container sheet aluminum, eventually become items found in everyday use, such as beverage cans, food packages, and pharmaceutical packaging. The plant also produces aluminum blanks, which are used to form cookware, automotive parts, snow shovels, grain scoops, and light reflectors. Aluminum sheet from the plant is used for automotive air-conditioning evaporators and aluminum coil for automotive trim.

A former manager of the Lancaster plant, George Stoe is now president of Alumax Mill Products, Inc. Stoe envisions continued growth for the company as it searches for new markets and develops new aluminum products. "We have found great success and many market leadership positions by concentrating our production efforts in specialized areas," he says. "Maintaining a low-cost, highly productive business, paying attention to our customers, and exploring growth opportunities gives us what we need to preserve our various value-added leadership positions."

The cold rolling mills.

One of the first buildings at the Manheim Pike site.

High Industries, Incorporated

High Industries' original home on West Lemon Street, Lancaster.

It was a risky business the High brothers started in 1931, at the height of the Great Depression. Jobs were scarce when Sanford and Benjamin High purchased a small welding shop on West Lemon Street, in Lancaster.

Giving their customers "good measure," they threw their combined energies into making the shop successful. They pioneered the concept of welding bridges rather than using the traditional hot rivet method. When the state gave them the opportunity to prove their welding on a York County bridge in 1933, it opened the door for the steel bridge repair and construction that continues to be the heart of the firm's business to this day.

Ben High left the business to start his own welding shop in 1937. By 1941 Sanford had moved into a new and much larger shop at James and Water streets, and the company was up to 12 employees.

Through the 1940s the company did a variety of work, from the repair of bulldozers and farm equipment to the manufacture of farm wagons, fire engines, and storage tanks. In 1946 the company completed its first major project involving fabrication and erection of structural steel—a bridge over the Delaware River.

A new plant was built along the Old Philadelphia Pike at Greenfield Road in 1954. Business was good through the 50s, and the firm incorporated as High Welding Company in 1956. In addition to steel for bridges, High Welding also supplied and erected structural steel for a number of area high schools.

The 60s and 70s were decades of steady growth, not only in steel but also into businesses such as precast concrete, commercial and residential real estate, and construction.

The commercial real estate portion of the business grew to become High Associates, Ltd., which now manages and leases apartments, as well as commercial/industrial facilities, including the Greenfield Corporate Center—a modern commercial development that is home to nearly 150 businesses and includes a large park area open to the public.

Today, High Industries, Inc., has diversified to include hotel management, food service, temporary employee services, and the operation of a steel service center.

The corporation is in its second generation of family management, with S. Dale High as president and Calvin G. High as senior vice president.

The High philosophy for conducting business states, in part, that the company will not only continue to give "good measure," as its founders had done, but will also build trustworthy relationships, be an innovative leader, and contribute to a world of beauty, peace, and prosperity.

Federal-Mogul Corporation

Although the Lititz plant of the Federal-Mogul Corporation is part of an international corporation with $2 billion in annual sales, it had humble beginnings in 1898 as the Star Ball Retainer Company.

Star Ball Retainer was organized by D. H. Keiper of Lancaster to manufacture a unique, ball bearing retainer. The product was used mainly for wheels on bicycles, a primary mode of transportation in those days. As automobiles came on the scene, the market for ball bearing products expanded. To accommodate the increased demand, Star Ball Retainer merged with the Bretz Company, an importer and seller of ball bearing products, in 1913 and was renamed the Bearings Company of America. In 1953 Bearings was acquired by Federal-Mogul. At the time, the company had 610 employees and 121,000 square feet of manufacturing space on Harrisburg Avenue and Manheim Pike. It is now known as the Chassis Products Operation of Federal-Mogul.

Today, the 275,000-square-foot plant in Lititz employs 450 workers and produces ball bearing assemblies for the automobile, farm implement, and construction equipment industries. Built at a cost of $65 million, the Lititz plant produced its first ball bearing product on January 2, 1987. Its production lines contain the most modern, state-of-the-art equipment. (The Harrisburg Avenue plant has been sold to Franklin & Marshall College, which will use the building in its campus expansion.)

The Manheim Pike facility was recently refurbished and acquired new, precision machining equipment in order to bring work in-house that had previously been sent to outside contractors.

When Federal-Mogul decided to build a new plant to enlarge its ball bearing products manufacturing facilities, it could have chosen to move closer to its customers' factory locations. It chose, instead, to remain in Lancaster County, according to Ken Herr, plant superintendent of the local operation, because of the superb work force here. "We have expertise and experience here that you just can't find elsewhere. Many of our employees have over 30 years with the company."

Steelworkers Local 1035 has represented the plant workers for 55 years, and Herr is proud of the good relationship between labor and management at the Lititz and Lancaster facilities. In fact, the company received the Pennsylvania Governor's Award for Labor and Management Relations for 1991.

The plant operates on the team concept, with each team responsible for all phases of production in their area of the plant; even arranging the location of manufacturing equipment within their area.

The Lititz plant of Federal-Mogul has a significant competitive advantage in the industry, thanks to its modern facilities and excellent employees. The plant looks forward to a continuation in its trends of increasing sales and expanding its work force.

Federal-Mogul's original plant, located on Harrisburg Avenue, pictured here in the late 1940s.

Serta Mattress Company Div. of Herr Manufacturing Co.

John K. Herr.

A third of a person's life is spent in bed, and since people spend that much time on a mattress, they want a good one. John K. Herr, Sr., knew this fact when he started his mattress company in 1907, on the third floor of a small building on South Christian Street, in Lancaster. He was determined to make a good mattress.

He certainly spared no effort in making one. At that time the regular work week was 59 hours, and there were only three people in the work force. Mattresses stuffed with straw and corn husks were then the most popular products, but they were soon replaced with ones filled with cotton felt, hair, and kapok.

As the business grew, careful attention was paid to the changing demands of customers. The firm was a pioneer in the manufacture and sale of innerspring mattresses and has remained in the forefront of the industry in product design and development.

When the company was started in 1907, it was one of five local mattress makers. Today it remains the only continuously operated mattress manufacturer in Lancaster County. In 1929 Herr and 14 other mattress manufacturers founded Serta, Inc., to pool advertising, purchasing power, and ideas. Each company developed its own area of primary responsibility, and this new organization helped the group through the depression years.

During World War II production dropped as the economy shifted away from the manufacture of consumer products. In 1942 the company was reorganized from John Herr's sole ownership to a partnership with his daughter and three sons. When the war ended, America went on a building boom, and mattress sales also rose. By 1953 the old plant was too small, and a new plant was built at the company's present location on Fountain Avenue. At that time the company was reorganized as Serta Mattress Company, Division of Herr Manufacturing Co.

The company continues to grow as one of 28 Serta factories in the United States. However, it has remained a locally owned family business, and management has passed to the third generation. Herr Manufacturing Co. remains a major contributor to the Serta organization, frequently winning awards for the quality of its products. That's no surprise, because the company's objectives clearly state: "Quality is our most important product. Service is our most important job." This level of achievement is attained through the contributions of all the company's associates who strive to manufacture the highest-quality products possible.

As an innovator in the bedding industry, Herr Manufacturing Company continues to uphold the tradition and philosophies of its founder, John K. Herr, Sr., offering quality products at reasonable prices.

Cassey Engerineering Co., Inc.

The sign in front of a modest building on Main Street in Salunga, Pennsylvania, gives almost no indication of what is taking place inside. Behind those walls, a small group of mechanical engineers create complex machines that have never been made before.

When Cassey Engineering was challenged, for instance, to design a mechanical orthopedic hospital bed, the firm came up with one that had two major advantages over anything in use at the time. The Cassey-designed bed could be moved quickly into the critically important Trendellenberg position directly from any other configuration. Other orthopedic beds in use at the time had to first be returned to the level starting point, losing precious seconds in the life of a heart patient.

The mechanical bed was also designed to operate while carrying up to 1,000 pounds. This was done to accommodate the added weight of water-bed mattresses now required for some patients.

Throughout the firm's 30-year history, it has designed automated production-line equipment for the candy and packaging industries, dump containers for waste management, an automatic pretzel oven, a machine to automatically perform the process of purifying molten aluminum, and a motorized machine that removes old shingles, tar paper, and nails from an inclined roof, delivering the debris directly to pick-up trucks with special air filter enclosures attached to the standard pick-up beds.

Harold Cassey, founder and owner of the firm, always had ability with machines and always wanted to go into business for himself. He started designing special machines in 1963, working from his home in Landisville. The young engineering business struggled in its early years, and Cassey took night jobs to make ends meet.

Within five years, he knew his engineering firm would be successful. There was a need for machines to increase productivity, and he could design them. Cassey Engineering moved to its present location in 1974, hired its first employee, and has enjoyed steady growth ever since.

"What we do here is use common sense to solve problems for people," Cassey explained. "Engineering principles haven't changed; something mechanical still has to do the work. We use computers only to guide and control that work."

A startling new real-life, computerized amusement ride, designed by Cassey, known as the "Chameleon," will soon be showing up at theme parks around the world. Based on principles used in military flight simulators, Chameleon has 10 totally enclosed gondolas rotating on 20-foot-long arms around a center point. Operators in the gondolas select their own adventure, flying an F-18 jet plane off an aircraft carrier, driving a Formula One race car at 200 miles an hour, or guiding a speeding offshore power boat, among others.

Any motion-based experience can be programmed into Chameleon's software to provide realistic simulation through actual movement of the gondola combined with 3-D computer graphic imaging. Chameleon lets each driver interactively determine the outcome of the ride.

Harold Cassey says his company, which now employs 12 engineers, "makes unconventional things through the use of orthodox engineering. How you think in this business," he says, "is what counts."

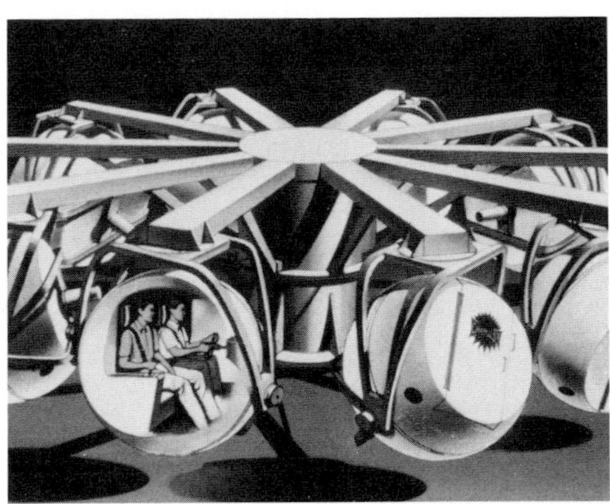

Designed and engineered by Cassey Engineering, the Chameleon is a high-tech computerized amusement ride that allows the operator to experience all the thrills of operating a speedboat, a race car, a jet aircraft, and other fast-moving machines.

The present site of Cassey Engineering in Salunga housed Heistand Hardware, the Salunga Post Office, and a soda fountain at the turn of the century.

Lancaster Laboratories

Founder Earl Hess, foreground, stands near the entrance to Lancaster Laboratories, constructed in 1991. With him are, from left, Kenneth E. Hess, executive vice president, finance and data processing; Carol D. Miller, executive vice president, human resources and administration; and J. Wilson Hershey, executive vice president, laboratory operations. Photo by Lancaster Newspapers, Inc.

In 1961 the walls went up for a new building along the New Holland Pike just east of Lancaster. The small, red-brick building was the home of Lancaster Laboratories, a company originally established to provide scientific services to agriculture-related businesses. The founders of the fledgling business were willing to invest the hard work needed to make Lancaster Laboratories a success—and their efforts and vision eventually paid off.

The founders were Dr. Earl Hess and his wife, Anita. The Hesses put their house on the line, and two professional colleagues—Dr. Christoph Grundmann and Dr. Ray Dawson—each put up $5,000 to help finance the new company.

The company founders were intent on using their wealth of knowledge and experience to find new ways to improve agricultural production, to use crop by-products, and to improve food processing. This required visits to farmers, mills, manufacturers, food processors, and other agricultural enterprises to learn about their needs.

"We weren't sure just what we could be doing for farmers and agri-businesses, but we were certain there were many beneficial applications for our scientific backgrounds just waiting for us to discover them," Hess recalls.

Although he didn't know it at the time, the young entrepreneur was following one of the underlying principles of a process now known as Total Quality Management—striving to fully understand and satisfy client requirements.

What Hess found on his visits was a wide range of problems and opportunities that would put the company's analytical skills and ingenuity to the test. In the early years Lancaster Laboratories used its scientific expertise in research for some the area's best-known industries. Projects ranged from alfalfa-pelleting experiments for a farm-equipment manufacturer and development of a cocoa-shell extraction process, to helping improve two of the area's most famous foods—soft pretzels and Lebanon bologna.

The small staff's hard work and commitment to quality and personal service began to result in a loyal core of clients. In 1965 there was sufficient business to justify a 900-square-foot addition.

By 1970 a dozen people were working on various research and development projects, as well as analytical procedures. The company had found its niche: providing high-quality technical information with third-party objectivity.

As the business grew, so did Hess' belief that the future of the company was directly tied to its employees. One's technical competence was simply not enough to become part of Lancaster Laboratories. Employees had to share in the commitment to quality service. Hess realized that, in return, the company had to support and enrich the lives of its employees.

Lancaster Laboratories employees enjoy a wide range of training, career guidance, and family-oriented benefits programs. Realizing that some people have more aptitude in technical areas than in management positions, Hess believes in providing development opportunities for either career path.

Just as the company evolved over the years, so the founder's role grew from one of scientist to manager to small business advocate and leader on local, state, and national levels. From 1984 to 1986, Hess served as president of the American Council of Independent Laboratories. In 1985 he was chairman of the board of the Lancaster Chamber of Commerce and Industry, and in 1986, he chaired the Pennsylvania delegation to the White House Conference on Small Business. From 1991 to 1994, he served as Eastern Region vice chair of the U.S. Chamber of Commerce.

In 1988 he was named Pennsylvania Business Leader of the Year by the Pennsylvania Chamber of Business and Industry, and in the same year he received the Exemplar Award from the Lancaster Chamber and the Alumni Citation from Franklin and Marshall College. In 1992 he was named an ACIL Fellow by the American Council of Independent Laboratories.

Near the end of 1991 Hess announced his desire to transfer the day-to-day chief operating responsibilities to an Executive Group made up of three executive vice presidents. He remains chairman of the board and chief executive officer, focusing on strategic planning. He plans to spend much of his time promoting dialogue among business, religious, and environmental groups.

Today, after more than 32 years of innovative business development, Lancaster Laboratories has grown into a company campus that includes a 115,800-square-foot laboratory facility, a workshop, a barn, an outdoor pavilion for employee use, and child-care, adult-day-care, and fitness centers. The company offers analytical services to clients in the western part of the country through its affiliated laboratory, Mountain States Analytical, Inc., in Salt Lake, Utah.

Lancaster Laboratories and its people have become recognized leaders among independent labs, pioneering a wide range of technologies. For example, the computerized Laboratory Information Management System (LIMS) was developed there. LIMS has since been adopted internationally by leading laboratories. A new robotic sample-retrieval system using bar codes, which Hess describes as a major laboratory breakthrough, was also designed and installed at Lancaster Laboratories.

With annual sales of about $26 million, Lancaster Laboratories is the nation's largest environmental laboratory that is privately held by the same people who founded it. The company also provides analytical services in the food and pharmaceutical sciences. Its 470-plus employee family puts it in the top 10 percent of independent commercial laboratories in the United States and among the top 50 employers in Lancaster County.

The company now serves a diverse range of businesses and industries in North, Central, and South America, Europe, Japan, and Australia, as well as federal, state, and local governments throughout the United States. Clients include more than 60 of the *Fortune* 100 companies.

Often cited for its family-friendly policies, the laboratory received honorable mention in Harvard's George S. Dively award for corporate public initiative in 1992 and was named to *Inc.* magazine's "Best Small Companies to Work for" list in 1993. Lancaster Laboratories, "Where Quality is a Science," has steadfastly clung to its motto.

Indeed, the one thing that has remained constant since the very beginning is the company's corporate philosophy of providing high-quality technical data with personal service at a fair fee and in an ethical manner. Lancaster Laboratories is living proof of Hess' view that "if you focus on doing things right, in the right way, profits will follow automatically."

A small brick building was the first home of Lancaster Laboratories. Since 1961 this building has been expanded to a total of 115,800 square feet with nine separate additions.

Tara Spaide (foreground), senior technician/coordinator, and Brian Corrie, senior technician, assemble liquid-to-liquid extractors for sample analyses in one of the company's laboratories.

Burnham Corporation

The original Burnham boiler plant in Irvington, New York, before the turn of the century.

The hot water and steam heating equipment for which the Burnham Corporation is so well known today grew out of the need to heat greenhouses more than 100 years ago. Frederick A. Lord began building greenhouses in 1856. His son-in-law, William A. Burnham, became his partner in 1872, and one year later the Lord & Burnham Company began producing cast-iron boilers in Irvington, New York.

Residential heating quickly became a major market for the firm's boilers, so the Lord & Burnham Boiler Department was created in 1895. Steel boilers were added to the line, and in 1919 the Burnham Boiler Corporation was formed to take over the boiler business of Lord & Burnham.

As sales of hydronic (hot water or steam) heating equipment increased, a foundry and machine shop was built in Lancaster Pennsylvannia in 1923 for the production of cast-iron boilers.

During World War II, a new steel-products plant in Lancaster was used to assist the war effort, producing pontoon bridges, handgrenade casings, and aircraft carrier decks.

After the war, new boiler designs and more efficient production methods were introduced by Burnham Boiler. The company developed "Baseray"® cast-iron baseboard radiation, the first of its kind. During this period Burnham introduced the packaged, or factory-assembled, boiler concept to the industry.

The Lord & Burnham Company and Burnham Boiler Company merged in 1947 to become Burnham Corporation. Penn Boiler and Burner Company of Lancaster, a leading manufacturer of residential steel boilers, was acquired by Burnham in 1968. The company's Lancaster facility has since been expanded and modernized to maintain its position as an industry leader.

Burnham now makes Lancaster its corporate headquarters and operates three production facilities, a distribution center, and an engineering center in the city. All castings for Burnham boilers are made in the firm's Zanesville, Ohio, plant. Products are shipped nationwide from Burnham's Lancaster distribution center.

Modern Burnham boilers range from residential units small enough to heat three-room apartments, to commercial boilers capable of heating multi-story buildings. Today's boilers are fired by gas, oil, or a combination of the two, as well as by electricity and solid fuels.

Burnham is the only full-line boiler manufacturer in the United States. It is also the only domestic manufacturer that produces all of its own boiler and hydronic-radiation castings. The corporation today includes, as wholly owned subsidiaries, New York Boiler Company, Inc., Colmar Pennsylvania; Kewanee Manufacturing Company, Inc., Kewanee, Illinois; and Governale Company, Inc., Brooklyn, New York.

Burnham boilers are the acknowledged leaders in their industry, having earned a reputation for continuing innovation. Many of the company's product designs have been industry firsts, including baseboard radiation, tri-fuel boilers, packaged boilers, and microprocessor controls.

Burnham's hydronic research and engineering tradition has enabled the firm to provide its customers with the most efficient, safe, and dependable hydronic heating systems available today.

Burnham Corporation's present headquarters in Lancaster, Pennsylvania.

Ford New Holland

In 1895 when Abe Zimmerman opened a repair shop in New Holland, he could not have known the business would grow to become one of the world's largest farm and industrial equipment manufacturers.

Zimmerman immediately started making his own New Holland brand of feed mills, followed by a gasoline engine with a water jacket that would not freeze in winter. He incorporate his small business in 1903, the same year a man named Henry Ford also incorporated his Michigan company for the manufacture of automobiles.

The New Holland Machine Company prospered until the Great Depression and the coming of rural electrification combined to cut deeply into the sale of the firm's products. But in 1940, the company was purchased by a group of four men who had an exciting new machine to build. Henry Fisher, George Delp, Irl Daffin, and Raymond Buckwalter obtained the rights to manufacture and sell the world's first successful automatic pick-up, self-tying hay baler.

Invented by Ed Nolt, a local thresherman, the hay baler was immediately accepted by farmers. Succeeding models of the baler now used around the world have been manufactured continuously in New Holland since 1940.

The "Machine Company," as it was known locally, was acquired by the Sperry Corporation in 1947. Through the years, a long line of machinery was developed, and Sperry New Holland became a world leader in harvesting equipment.

Even as the New Holland story was unfolding, Henry Ford was applying his genius to the development of a tractor that would eventually replace horsepower on the farm. The first Fordson tractor was introduced by Henry Ford and Son, of Dearborn, Michigan, in 1917. It became the first inexpensive, mass-produced tractor on the market.

Ford tractors pioneered the use of rubber pneumatic tires, power hydraulics, and diesel engines. Then in 1939, the immediately popular and now famous Model 9N tractor hit the market and changed agriculture forever.

The 9N introduced the first three-point hitch, now standard on all tractors. It allowed implements to be easily attached directly to the tractor and to be raised and lowered hydraulically. It also allowed the Ford tractor to do the work of tractors twice its weight. So popular was the 9N that even now, more than 50 years later, it is still not uncommon to find them operating on farms.

Ford Tractor and New Holland came together as part of Ford Motor Company in 1987, with the worldwide headquarters of the new company located in New Holland.

In 1991, Fiat of Italy and Ford Motor Company completed an agreement that brought their worldwide tractor, farm, and industrial equipment operations together under a new holding company named N.H. Geotech n.v., 80 percent owned by Fiat and 20 percent owned by Ford. In January 1993, N.H. Geotech was renamed New Holland, n.v., and during that same summer, Fiat assumed entire ownership. With North American headquarters in New Holland, the company is now a global giant, producing more tractors than any other company and ranking among the world's top three farm and industrial equipment companies.

Inventor Ed Nolt of Lancaster County made this prototype in 1937 of what would become the world-famous New Holland hay baler.

J.L. Clark, Inc.

A sampling of the decorative metal cans made by J.L. Clark.

In 1919, less than one year after the armistice ending World War I, Adam and Seymour Batdorf founded the Liberty Sign and Can Company in Lancaster. The county had long been known for its pretzels, potato chips, and cigar tobacco, so it's not surprising to find a company equally well known for manufacturing the lithographed metal cans in which those products are sold.

In addition to decorated cans and boxes, Liberty also produced metal signs for business. The company grew to 200 employees and annual sales of $2,500,000 by 1955. Looking toward retirement, the Batdorf brothers sold the company to another lithographer and can maker, the J.L. Clark Company of Rockford, Illinois.

John Lewis Clark, the founder of J.L. Clark and its modern successor, CLARCOR, was a tinsmith who made his living as a hardware merchant at the turn of the century. In November of 1904 he opened a modest metal lithographing operation in Rockford, chartered as the J.L. Clark Manufacturing Company. His first product was a decorative metal flue stopper, and was soon followed by ointment boxes flour sifters, and toasters.

Under J.L. Clark leadership, the Lancaster division grew its original business, and by 1964 new products were added, including metal containers for spices, throat lozenges, bandages, and ink stamp pads.

A J.L. Clark plant in Havre de Grace, Maryland, was consolidated into the Lancaster Division in 1986, increasing the local plant's spice and tobacco can business, taking it to sales of nearly $30 million a year, and employing over 250 people. Today, the company makes Band-Aid boxes, McCormack spice containers, and promotional cans for Hershey Chocolate, Nestle, and M&M Mars, as well as Kiwi shoe polish.

Another CLARCOR plant, located in Lancaster since 1974, is Clark Filter in the Hempfield Industrial Park. This company is the country's dominant manufacturer of lube and fuel filters for diesel locomotives. It has annual sales of over $10 million and employs more than 100 people in Lancaster.

Clark Filter is an outgrowth of the old Stone Industrial Corporation, purchased by Clark in 1971. Stone was the first manufacturer of spiral-wound drinking straws and later made paper and plastic tubes as well as pleated paper products.

J.L. Clark has always recognized the importance of its employees. The J.L. Clark Association, begun in 1919 at Rockford and now part of 20 CLARCOR operations worldwide, has served to bring employees together socially and to build a team environment. J.L. Clark continues to be committed to its customers, associates, and the Lancaster community.

Simon Ladder Towers, Inc.

If ever there was a company that used innovation to climb to the top of its industry, Simon Ladder Towers, Inc., is it. This company, founded less than 20 years ago, has become the world's leading manufacturer of aerial fire apparatus by taking a lot of climbing out of fire fighting and high-level rescues.

In the 1960s big city fire departments sought to develop hydraulic platforms to replace standard "hook and ladder" trucks. At the same time, smaller suburban communities, which had no ladder trucks, were showing an increased interest in them. (In 1970, Lancaster County fire companies had only six aerial trucks in use; today there are 15.) This was due to suburban building booms and a growing shortage of manpower in volunteer fire departments. The manpower shortage was important since it takes six men to raise a 50-foot ground ladder, while just one man can operate a 100-foot aerial device.

In 1974 a group of Lancaster County investors saw the possibilities in the new aerial platforms and formed Ladder Towers, Incorporated (LTI). Using rented space in Leola, LTI began manufacturing aerial ladders for use by other fire apparatus manufacturers.

Company engineers soon developed the world's first ladder tower unit designed for fire fighting. This allowed one man to operate a hydraulically controlled platform equipped with pre-piped water outlets, eliminating the need for fire fighters to climb high ladders while lugging heavy equipment. A ladder tower 100 feet tall or more could be mounted on a maneuverable straight chassis truck. The LTI design was a big hit with fire departments across the nation.

LTI soon decided to build aerial apparatus under its own name. A 113,000-square-foot plant and office complex near Ephrata was built to house the business, which had become international in scope. The modern plant has an automotive-quality paint facility capable of finishing fire apparatus to the rigid demands of the fire service. The company also became a major refurbisher of fire apparatus.

Simon-LTI aerial ladder in action.

By the mid-1980s LTI had become the nation's leading producer of aerial fire apparatus. It introduced a full line of aerial products on LTI-designed and -built Olympian chassis. It also introduced for use in airports the first crash rescue truck to be equipped with aerial ladders.

In 1987 Simon Engineering of the United Kingdom, a major worldwide manufacturer of fire apparatus and other products, acquired LTI. Simon-LTI has more than 250 employees in Lancaster County, 40 independent sales representatives throughout the U.S., and three regional service centers. Lancaster County-built Simon-LTI fire apparatus is sold worldwide by the Simon Group.

Further expansion of the company's line can be expected, since Simon LTI's mission statement calls for it to be "a world-class supplier of technologically advanced fire fighting apparatus."

Ladder Tower—McAllen Fire Department, Texas.

Lancaster Paint & Glass Company

The Lancaster Paint & Glass Company factory and store on North Prince Street in 1900.

Dave Harnish began making his own paints in Lancaster in 1884. A year later he opened a paint store in the first block of South Queen Street. By 1890 the young paint business had become successful enough that Harnish took on a partner, Abraham L. Leaman. The business was known simply as "Harnish and Leaman."

By 1896 the demand for paint and varnish had increased to the point that the store on South Queen Street was too small, so it was moved to larger quarters a few doors up the street to South Queen and Center Square, now Penn Square. At about the same time, Harnish and Leaman also opened a factory at 338 North Charlotte Street.

In October of 1900 Leaman retired. Harnish then formed The Lancaster Paint & Glass Company and opened a combined factory and store at 233-235 North Prince Street. The buildings were expanded to the rear to allow access to the Pennsylvania Railroad tracks, enabling easy delivery of the raw materials required in paint manufacturing.

Lancaster Ready-Mix Paint was the leading brand made and sold by the young company in its North Prince Street store at the turn of the century.

"Lancaster Ready-Mix Paint" was the leading brand made by the company. It was sold throughout Pennsylvania and surrounding states. The company also carried oils, varnishes, glass, cement, and a vast array of related paint and glass items. Brushes sold through the company were so popular they could be found in use as far away as New Mexico.

Lancaster Paint & Glass Company continued to prosper, providing paints and coatings to local manufacturing firms, which during this period were producing materials for two world wars. The company also produced a growing selection of paints for residential and commercial uses. Everything from carriage paints to automobile enamels, varnish stains, graining combs, blackboard paint, cement paint, sealers, and putty were manufactured at the Lancaster plant.

As the county grew, Lancaster Paint & Glass Company supplied many of the outlying hardware and dry goods stores from its large inventory of products. But during the 1960s and 1970s, as compliance with a growing number of federal regulations required increasing amounts of investment in equipment, paint manufacturing gradually decreased, and the company began direct purchases from large paint manufacturers. Paint was still distributed to customers at both the wholesale and retail levels.

Lancaster Paint & Glass Company continued to "paint" Lancaster as it played a significant roll in the development of original color palettes for projects such as Old Town Lancaster and other historic restoration work.

As architectural changes called for the increased use of metal and glass in construction, the company expanded its window glass, mirror glass, and glazing operations. Then in 1984 it stopped selling paint to concentrate entirely on the glass, mirror, and plastic business.

With the largest selection of glass, specialty glass, mirror glass, and plastic in Lancaster County, Lancaster Paint & Glass Company has made a proud contribution to the growth of the area and is now in its second hundred years supplying the best in quality, price, and service.

Althouse, Martin & Associates, Inc.

One of the most visible signs of growth in Lancaster County—The Greenfield Corporate Center—can be seen from its busiest highway. The range of impressive structures there catches the eyes of millions of motorists each year and thousands of employees and visitors each day.

Designing those modern buildings to meet the needs of tenants while blending them in with neighboring structures has been the work of an architectural firm that had its beginnings in an old stone farmhouse built in 1795. All but two Greenfield structures were designed by Althouse, Martin & Associates, Inc. The firm began business in 1966, in the historic Kimmel house, which is on the National Register of Historic Places.

A quarter-century, hundreds of projects, and a world of changes have shaped the Althouse, Martin story. Despite these many changes, the firm has stuck to its founding principles by maintaining excellent communications with clients, technical consultants, and the construction industry. It is through such communication that functional, aesthetically appropriate design solutions are found.

The firm's success and recognition for outstanding work didn't come overnight. Many hours were spent in the small office at the rear of Harold H. Althouse's historic home. Things got crowded when John H. Martin joined the firm in 1969 and even more cramped when B. Kevin Johnson joined in 1973.

But they loved their work and took on many small projects, striving to meet deadlines—and always stressing the importance of communicating with all involved; therefore becoming a very successful firm.

Architects didn't advertise in those days, but word of their talent and reliability got around the industry. Bigger jobs began to come their way.

John H. Martin, right, and B. Kevin Johnson in front of the Charter House, left, and the Shoppes at Greenfield, right.

The results speak for themselves in the design of the massive Skyline Distributors distribution center and the expansion of Donecker's Restaurant in Ephrata; in financial buildings, like the award-winning Meridian Bank in downtown Lancaster and the Bank of Lancaster County main headquarters in Greenfield Corporate Center; in the four-story High Associates, Ltd., headquarters and the copper-roofed Shoppes at Greenfield; and in the conversion of the old Nichols Department Store building on Manheim Pike into the attractive City Line Business Center.

Althouse, Martin & Associates, Inc., has been a part of the architectural profession's move from pencils and drawing boards to highly sophisticated computer-design techniques. But the architects' training, experience, and love of creating functional, pleasing structures has enhanced the power of the firm's computer-aided design system.

With its office in the Greenfield Corporate Center, Althouse, Martin & Associates, Inc., plans to be an important part of Lancaster County's future.

Althouse, Martin & Associates, Inc., design striking new structures.

Wickersham Construction and Engineering, Inc.

Col. John H. Wickersham.

Young John H. Wickersham learned early about his future in the family printing business. His father, owner of Wickersham Printing in Lancaster, told the son there was no place for him in the firm, and that he would have to go out and "make your own way in the world."

So John went to Yale University where he earned a degree in civil engineering. After graduation he worked in Connecticut and New York, gaining experience on major projects such as the Lincoln Tunnel.

He returned to Lancaster and founded his own building construction firm in 1906. At about the same time, he and his father visited the scene of the 1904 Baltimore fire to determine what buildings had withstood the flames. They observed that structures made of reinforced concrete, a new idea in construction at the time, had come through the fire intact.

Armed with this new knowledge, John proceeded to construct a reinforced concrete building for his father's printing business—a building still standing and in use in the second block of East Chestnut Street, Lancaster.

When the first reinforced concrete beam for that building had been poured in place, Wickersham's carpenters were afraid it would crumble under its own weight, and they refused to climb out onto it to remove the wooden forms. So the colonel picked up a sledge hammer, went out onto the beam himself, and proceeded to knock off the wooden forms. Before long his men followed him onto the obviously safe beam and finished the work.

Convinced of this new product's superiority, Wickersham made his company, John H. Wickersham Engineering and Construction, Inc., a local pioneer in the use of reinforced concrete for major structures.

In those early days of reinforced concrete, clients were often skeptical of its ability to safely span a wide space, but Wickersham could usually persuade them with the simple logic that, "You don't think I would have used it for my own father if it was not the best?"

During World War I Wickersham was in the U.S. Army Corps of Engineers, serving with General Pershing's headquarters in the European theater and rising to the rank of lieutenant colonel. He later became a full colonel in the army reserves, a title that stayed with him for the rest of his life.

After the war a good friend, Milton Hershey, invited Wickersham to build him a large factory in a new town that was growing up around Hershey's thriving chocolate candy business. Wickersham was told to put up just one building. Hershey's own people would observe and then construct all subsequent buildings themselves.

The first building was completed, but Hershey's attempt to enter the construction trade proved less successful than his candy business. So the following year, and for a number of years thereafter, Wicker-

Wickersham's management, from left: Brad Ford Smith, vice president, estimating; Albert Mauger, president; and David Nace, vice president, construction.

sham constructed buildings for the fast-growing Hershey Chocolate Company.

Before starting work on a Hershey building, Wickersham would go to New York City and hire Italian immigrant laborers. Then, as each plant was completed, the workers would be offered permanent jobs with Hershey Chocolate Company and a welcome new start in America.

The relationship between Hershey and Wickersham Construction has continued through the years and succeeding generations of company management. In 1991 Wickersham completed a new corporate boardroom for Hershey, along with renovations to the corporate offices and to the firm's Reese Food facility.

Wickersham's early leadership in the use of reinforced concrete led to contracts for concrete bridge work on the original Pennsylvania Turnpike. The firm also constructed elevated railroad bridges for the Pennsylvania Railroad Company. Nearly all the bridges constructed by Wickersham are still in use, including the Lititz Pike bridge on the Route 30 bypass, north of Lancaster.

The longevity of the buildings designed and constructed by Wickersham can be attested to by their recently completed exterior renovations at the VF Factory Outlet Complex in Wyomissing. These renovations were the first major exterior repairs made to the buildings since their construction by J. H. Wickersham in 1915.

It is difficult, if not impossible, to travel far in Lancaster County without entering buildings constructed by the Wickersham firm. These structures stand as evidence of Wickersham Construction's involvement in the growth of business and industry in the area during the last 87 years.

In addition to buildings for Hershey Chocolate Company, Wickersham has a long construction history with Wilbur Chocolate in Lititz and Klien's Chocolate in Elizabethtown (now M&M/Mars). In Lancaster Wickersham lists among its projects plants built for the Bearings Company (now Federal-Mogul), Grinnell Corporation, and R. R. Donnelley, as well as for Lancaster Newspapers, Inc.

Original construction, Hershey Chocolate Company.

Institutional facilities have been completed in recent years for the Brethren Village Retirement Community in Neffsville, the Lancaster Theological Seminary, and both Lancaster General Hospital and St. Joseph Hospital.

The modern company, now in its fourth generation of management, has developed a solid reputation as a reliable design/build firm. In addition to its heavy concrete construction experience, Wickersham also provides construction management services, industrial services, equipment installation, and rigging services.

Brethren Village Retirement Community.

The SICO Company

A SICO Company fuel delivery truck.

Clarence Schock is the one to be credited for making the decisions that have shaped The SICO Company. Yet the seeds of the business go back to 1830—to a struggling coal, grain, and lumber business run by his father.

The Schocks entered the oil products business by chance. A Mount Joy dealer in kerosene had become a competitor for their anthracite coal customers, and Schock's company retaliated by going into the oil business. At that time the oil business meant buying and selling kerosene in wood barrels. The beginning of the enterprise that is known today as The SICO Company dates to 1876, when kerosene was sold wholesale by Schock within a 10-mile radius of Mount Joy.

In those days the only use for gasoline was in gasoline stoves, and it was sold primarily by dealers who sold the stoves. It was cheaper than kerosene, and supply exceeded demand. But that changed in the 1890s with the introduction of the internal combustion engine. Clarence Schock was the first dealer in the area to install curbside gasoline pumps for cars in 1914. He was

A Clarence Schock anti-slosh tank truck.

also the first dealer to use automotive delivery trucks. He also pioneered the use of tank trucks in place of the barrel-delivery wagons. Schock designed several "anti-slosh" tank trucks that reduced the shifting of their liquid loads as they traveled the hills of Lancaster County and hauled petroleum products from the company's deep-water port in Wilmington, Delaware.

Schock had been selling Texaco gasoline under the name Star Independent Oil Company, and other petroleum products under the name Schock Independent Oil Company. In 1941 the businesses merged and became the SICO Company. The most important aspect of the business was that it remained an independent dealer, free to buy its products from any refiner. Today The SICO Company is one of the largest branded distributors of Amoco gasoline and also distributes gasoline from Exxon, Atlantic, and Texaco. It is also one of the top 20 national distributors of Citgo lubricants, and sells Amoco lubricants as well.

The SICO Company employs 475 people, operating from its corporate office in Mount Joy and from division offices in Pennsylvania, Delaware, and New Jersey. In addition to serving 144 stations, it operates a chain of SICOserve convenience store/quick lube/car wash businesses. The SICO Company also sells and services heating and air conditioning equipment.

Clarence Schock always believed in helping the community that made his business possible. There were two ways he provided for this. One was insisting on keeping The SICO Company located in Mount Joy so it would provide employment for area residents. The second is The SICO Foundation. Originally established to provide money to school districts for capital projects, today the foundation gives thousands of dollars in scholarships to students who pursue baccalaureate degrees in area colleges.

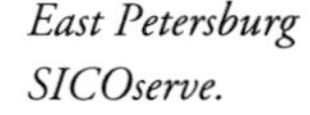
East Petersburg SICOserve.

A 5-gallon hand pump.

Pennsylvania Power & Light

After decades of occupying Lancaster's famous Greist Building, PP&L consolidated its operations into a new state-of-the-art division headquarters facility.

To this generation of Lancaster residents, Pennsylvania Power & Light Co. is the only power company in the city; but when Thomas Edison brought electricity to Pennsylvania in the 1880s, more than a few companies were vying to supply the area with energy.

One by one, they either went out of business or were merged with one another in often-circuitious ways. And, just as the hundreds of electric companies across Pennsylvania were narrowed down to the 11 investor-owned utilities that cover the state today, the dozens of companies in Lancaster eventually cast their lot with what was to become PP&L.

The earliest known power supplier in Lancaster was the Maxim Electric Light Co., which was owned by Philadelphia investors and had a plant on Church Street, just east of South Duke.

Maxim began generating direct-current electricity in October 1883, with two 60-horsepower steam engines driving four generators. By November 1883 the company was supplying current to a grand total of 121 lamps in the city.

Maxim faded from the scene, however, and the Edison Electric Co. began generating DC current on September 18, 1886, as demand for power was skyrocketing in Lancaster. Edison powered a number of firsts in the city. The first public places to be lighted by electricity were the Old City Hotel, on the site of the former Wheatland Hotel, and the Fulton Opera House. The first private residence to be lighted electrically was the home of Edison's president, G. Frederick Sener. The first church in the city with electricity was Grace Lutheran Church. The first electric motor used in Lancaster was in the East King Street establishment of Rose Bros. and Hartman's, Umbrella Manufacturers; it had a capacity of five horsepower.

The alternating current we use today arrived in Lancaster in 1891, when the Edison Co. installed two 40-killowatt AC generators.

Edison Company's customers were later served by the Lancaster County Railway and Light Co. and the Lancaster Electric Light, Heat and Power Co., both of which were merged with Pennsylvania Power & Light in 1930.

Today, Lancaster's "power company," PP&L, serves more than one million customers in a 29-county area of central eastern Pennsylvania. The city is home to one of the company's five major divisions, and the PP&L employees who work and live in Lancaster County are active participants in many facets of the city's life.

The 7,500 employees of PP&L regard it as a privilege to serve the people of central eastern Pennsylvania with electricity. In the past 70 years they have worked for the area's economic development and community betterment. In that time, they have seen greater Lancaster grow and prosper, becoming one of the most desirable regions in the United States.

The lights have been on in Lancaster for 110 years. Pennsylvania Power & Light employees, "working toward a brighter tomorrow," are striving to ensure that they stay on.

UGI Gas Service

The task of illuminating American homes in 1882 belonged to candles, oil lamps, and coal gas lights, but a key invention led to the formation that year of United Gas Improvement Company in Philadelphia and promised a brighter future for everyone.

Coal gas could not match the brilliance of the 1879 Edison incandescent electric lamp, but a new process for making coal gas nearly doubled its candle power while lowering its cost.

Originally formed to produce and market the new-process coal gas, United Gas Improvement was soon deeply involved in the infant electrical industry as well. The company's growth was explosive from the start. By the turn of the century it owned utilities and gas works throughout the country.

In Lancaster, gas for home and street lighting in the 19th century was being supplied by the Lancaster City Gas Company and Lancaster Gas Light and Fuel Company. The two merged in 1879 and eventually bought out the Edison Electric Illumination Company, which had brought electric power to the city in 1880.

It wasn't until 1949 that the United Gas Improvement Company, by that time known as UGI, formed the Lancaster County Gas Company and acquired the gas properties then operated by Pennsylvania Power & Light Company. The purchase included a coal gas manufacturing plant on Conestoga Street near Farnum Field, the site of UGI's Lancaster headquarters today.

In 1953 UGI brought the first natural gas to Lancaster. Lights and stoves were quickly adapted to use the new, safer gas that doubled the heating value of coal gas.

With natural gas came industrial growth as manufacturers were provided with a dependable source of gas for their heating processes. Today, UGI maintains nearly 1,000 miles of gas main in the city and county of Lancaster, serving over 38,000 residential and industrial-commercial customers.

Turn-of-the-century office of the forerunner of UGI, at Grant and Chestnut streets, in Lancaster.

With 118 employees in Lancaster today, UGI has made a strong commitment to remain in the city, backing it with a $2-million investment in its Conestoga Street property. The company has also opened Lancaster's first-ever gas appliance gallery at the Lancaster Shopping Center.

UGI continues to grow throughout Lancaster County, opening new areas to natural gas service every year. Non-corrosive plastic pipe is now used for all gas lines, and nearly all older lines have been replaced with the safer plastic.

UGI can see the possibility of natural gas in everyone's future. From the traditional uses of gas for home heating, hot water, cooking, and lighting, technology has greatly increased its applications to include air-conditioning and co-generation. Also being designed for use in the near future are low-maintenance automobiles that run on natural gas. One such car is already being used by UGI in Lancaster.

With seemingly inexhaustible supplies of natural gas available, UGI in Lancaster County can continue to tell its customers that for cost, convenience, and comfort, natural gas is still their best energy buy.

Denver and Ephrata Telephone and Telegraph Company

Architect's rendering of the six-story Brossman Business Complex in Ephrata. Completed in 1993, it serves as the new company headquarters.

William F. Brossman had the best telephone service available in 1909. He shared a party line with 19 neighbors. A farmer in the Red Run area near Reamstown, he was also the agent for a fertilizer company. But when a large shipment of fertilizer arrived, he couldn't get through on the phone to notify his customers. A man of resolve, he knew what had to be done; he had to start his own telephone company.

By May 1911 the Denver and Ephrata Telephone and Telegraph Company was in business. With Brossman as president, the young company provided its customers with much-improved telephone service, and within a year business had grown to the point that a full-time manager was needed. Christian E. Eaby was hired. He served the company through years of rapid growth and prosperity.

Upon Brossman's death in 1944, Eaby was elected president. Two years later, he married the founder's eldest daughter, Bertha, who had left school teaching in 1913 to join her father's business.

William F. Brossman was joined by daughters, Anne (left) and Bertha, in the family telephone business.

In 1956, Christian Eaby died, and Bertha Brossman Eaby was elected president. As chairman and president, she led her company to the forefront of the communications industry at a time when women were almost unknown in corporate leadership positions.

Denver and Ephrata Telephone is now under the leadership of its fourth president. Anne Brossman Sweigart, Bertha Blair's younger sister, was elected president and chairman upon Blair's death in 1985.

The company has always been an innovator and leader in telephone service. As early as 1962 D and E pioneered "911" emergency service in Lancaster County. The first Mobile Telephone Service (MTS) in the county also originated with D and E in 1963. Cable TV was added in 1965 as a wholly owned subsidiary.

D and E is now the 35th-largest telephone company in the United States and serves 45,000 phone lines throughout northern Lancaster County and parts of Lebanon and Berks counties from Manheim to Adamstown.

A stunning new six-story building adjacent to the firm's office at 130 East Main Street, Ephrata, was completed in 1993. The Brossman Business Complex serves as the new headquarters of the company.

Also housed in the $12-million complex will be a restaurant, two theaters, office space, conference and meeting facilities, and a video teleconferencing center—the area's first two-way interactive teleconferencing facility. This ultra-modern technology will allow a meeting to be conducted by participants at various locations around the country without the need for any of them to travel. Both the people in attendance and any materials presented will be clearly seen by all participants at their own viewing locations.

Eighty-three years after it was founded, the Denver and Ephrata Telephone and Telegraph Company remains committed to providing quality service for its customers. One of the first in the state to install a digital fiber optic system, D and E has laid the groundwork for the sophisticated telephone service of the future.

Bank of Lancaster County, N. A.

Bank of Lancaster County has embraced hard work and personal service as the guiding principle for its 130 years of operation. As the oldest federally chartered bank in Lancaster County, it traces its history back to the time of the Civil War.

Shortly after President Abraham Lincoln signed the National Bank Act in 1863, a group of enterprising Lancaster County investors applied for a federal bank charter. First National Bank of Strasburg (today's Bank of Lancaster County) was organized on May 16, 1863, and received Charter No. 42. Thus, the first bank to be located south of Lancaster City opened its doors for business on August 5, 1863. John F. Herr was its president and Edward M. Eberman its first cashier.

The financial institution grew and prospered over the years. In 1958 the bank opened its second office at a location in Willow Street. Six more offices opened between 1970 and 1980. During this time it became apparent that the name, First National Bank of Strasburg, no longer reflected the whole area being served by the growing bank. As a result the name was changed to First National Bank of Lancaster County in 1980 to show the public that the bank was remaining a part of the county but had expanded its operations beyond Strasburg. The new name identified the bank's commitment and reflected the fact that decision-making management was to remain close to home.

In 1987 a one-bank holding company was formed, Sterling Financial Corporation. Its purpose was to prepare First National Bank of Lancaster for a future of progress, while still protecting the shared values believed to make it "The Better Bank." At the same time, the bank's name was shortened to Bank of Lancaster County, N.A. to further clarify its positioning in the market.

Bank of Lancaster County's holdings also include Town and Country Leasing, Inc., which leases vehicles and equipment locally and nationally. Services range from leasing to fleet and individual customers to leasing computer and communications equipment to major corporations. The twentieth and newest branch location opened at Willow Valley Manor North in late 1993.

The services offered by Bank of Lancaster County have expanded along with its service area. Bank of Lancaster County is dedicated to being aware of the diverse needs of all Lancaster County residents. The bank recognizes that its role as a corporate citizen includes making a variety of vital banking services available to people of all backgrounds.

John E. Stefan, president and CEO, credits the bank's continued success to its devotion to customer service at all levels of operation. "Many banks give lip service to being customer oriented. We, in fact, *are* customer oriented," Stefan explains. "We think that Bank of Lancaster County has a very important difference in their approach—treating customers as true people rather than numbers. We are sophisticated in the services we offer, and in the equipment which handles our bookkeeping and accounting, but we are still a very personal bank.

"My objective for Bank of Lancaster County, as we go forward, is to continue to be a community-oriented bank, even though we have surpassed $500 million in asset size, and there will be a day when we approach $1 billion in size. The ongoing operating guideline of our bank will continue to be treating our customers in a friendly and professional way. This personalized service will let them know that they are serviced by their own local, hometown bank."

John F. Herr (left), first president of First National Bank of Strasburg, now the Bank of Lancaster County, and E.M. Eberman, the first cashier.

Bank of Lancaster County has been in business for 130 years.

Fulton Bank

James K. Sperry, chairman and chief executive officer of Fulton Bank.

The commitment to community and conservative management philosophies laid down by its founders on a cold February day in Lancaster in 1882 have been the cornerstone of Fulton Bank's success. The business ethics and practices established by their early predecessors have enabled succeeding generations to guide Fulton Bank, practically unscathed, through wars and peace, panics and depression.

A growing, prospering financial organization with assets of nearly $1.4 billion, Fulton Bank has maintained its roots solidly in the Lancaster community. Its present colonial-style headquarters' building on Penn Square is less than a half-block from where the bank opened its first office over 110 years ago.

Fulton Bank today enjoys relationships with businesses and individuals that have spanned generations. The bank is an important financial resource instrumental to the economic vitality of which Lancaster County is justifiably proud.

(In 1982 Fulton Bank became an affiliate, and the primary asset, of Fulton Financial Corporation, a $2.4-billion multi-bank holding company, which now operates six financial institutions in 10 Pennsylvania counties. Fulton Financial is rated among the best-performing and safest bank holding companies in the country.)

By maintaining excellent profitability, exceptional capital adequacy ratios, and exemplary asset quality, Fulton Bank is testimony to the fact that success comes to those who will not have their energies diverted from their primary objective. For the management of Fulton Bank that objective is operating an employee-sensitive, community-oriented, customer-responsive, shareholder-attractive financial institution.

Fulton Bank has an unflagging commitment to Lancaster County, as its people, its commerce, and its agriculture move toward the 21st century together.

One Penn Square, Lancaster headquarters of Fulton Bank.

CoreStates Hamilton Bank

CoreStates Hamilton Bank had its beginnings in a rented house at 41 North Queen Street, just a few doors from its present headquarters building. The year was 1810, the nation was on the brink of a second war with England, and Lancaster was the largest inland town in the nation. With 5,000 people and a bustling agricultural, commercial, and manufacturing economy, the borough needed a bank.

On January 17, leading citizens drew up articles of incorporation for Farmers Bank of Lancaster. Shares sold for $50 each and were parceled out among the county's larger towns so there could be a broad spectrum of participation. Familiar names from throughout the county, like Atlee, Bachman, Baer, Brenneman, Groff, Hager, Herr, Landis, Steinman, Watt, Witmer, and others, were associated with the bank in the early days.

In 1813, shortly before the British were setting fire to the new Capitol in Washington, D.C., the bank was moving into its new home at Duke and King streets. For more than 150 years the bank served the financial needs of the county from that office.

In 1963 the Farmers Bank and Lancaster County National Bank merged into Lancaster County Farmers National Bank. Consolidation continued for the remainder of the decade, with various banks in York, Harrisburg, and Reading creating National Central Bank in 1970.

CoreStates Hamilton Bank was the successor formed in 1980, taking its name from men who were involved in the formation of the nation, the city, and local industry. In 1983 the bank became a wholly owned subsidiary of CoreStates Financial Corp, which has total assets of $23 billion.

CoreStates Hamilton Bank employees' training and keen sense of professionalism are major ingredients in the bank's formula for success. Knowledge, product information, and service to customers play a key role in all retail, trust, and corporate banking services.

Innovation and the use of technology are also a powerful part of the mix. For example, CoreStates developed the MAC automated teller machine system, now part of Electronic Payment Services, Inc. More than 27 million cardholders from more than 1,450 participating financial institutions conduct more than 88 million transactions a month through MAC machines. MAC point-of-sale transactions are increasing dramatically. Home banking services, possible through personal computers, also provide opportunities for better, more convenient customer service.

CoreStates Hamilton Bank is community-oriented, encouraging employees to become involved in volunteer activities. Each year, employees contribute thousands of hours and enormous talent to more than 250 civic, service, and cultural organizations in the area.

Today CoreStates Hamilton Bank has 19 offices in Lancaster County, 64 offices in a six-county trade area, and a staff of 1,300 employees. Locally managed, its affiliation with CoreStates allows Hamilton Bank to meet the largest financial requirements worldwide for industrial, commercial, and individual customers.

The first home of CoreStates Hamilton Bank.

CoreStates Hamilton Bank headquarters, at 100 North Queen Street.

Dauphin Deposit Bank

Columbia National Bank.

The Susquehanna River, between Lancaster and York counties, was a major barrier to business and travel at the turn of the 19th Century. When the Columbia Bridge Company was formed in 1812 to span the river with a wooden structure, the sale of stock in the company brought in more funds than were required to complete the project.

A wooden, covered toll bridge was completed across the river in 1814, and officers of the company quickly decided everyone's investment would be best served by using the excess funds to offer banking services in the community. As banking laws were refined, the Columbia Bridge Company found it necessary to petition the state legislature to obtain official banking status, and in 1824 the corporation became the Columbia Bank and Bridge Company.

Banking eventually emerged as the primary activity of the corporation, and by the 1850s the bridge had become a separate business owned by the bank. This arrangement lasted until the Civil War when Union troops took possession of the bridge in the face of an advancing Confederate army. Then, just three days before the Battle of Gettysburg, Union soldiers were ordered to burn the bridge to prevent the enemy from crossing the river and invading Lancaster County.

New Holland Farmers National Bank.

For the next 40 years, numerous attempts to obtain reimbursement for the bridge from the U.S. government proved futile. It was also during this time that Columbia Bank and Bridge became known as Columbia National Bank and, later, as The First Columbia National Bank.

In 1923 the bank moved to its present location at Fourth and Locust streets, and in 1965 it was purchased by the Lancaster County Farmers National Bank. The present owner, Dauphin Deposit Bank and Trust Company, bought the Columbia office in 1970 and has owned it ever since.

Dauphin Deposit has enjoyed its own colorful history, opening in 1835 as the Harrisburg Savings Institution. The Borough of Harrisburg at that time did not yet even have a railroad station.

The bank prospered from the start. It became Dauphin Deposit Bank in 1845, with the name evolving through the years to its present form as Dauphin Deposit Bank and Trust Company in 1977.

Dauphin Deposit's growth into Lancaster County started with the Columbia Bank. Then in 1987 it purchased the assets of the New Holland Farmers National Bank, giving the new owners two locations in New Holland, as well as branch banks in Smoketown, Intercourse, and Manheim Township.

The New Holland bank had first opened for business in 1907, offering customers loans at five percent—a rate that remained unchanged with the bank for more than 50 years. Serving a farming community, the bank's original operating hours were from 7 a.m. to 5 p.m., Monday through Saturday.

Dauphin Deposit today has grown to become a major regional bank operating in Dauphin, Lancaster, Cumberland, York, Lebanon, Berks, Northampton, and Lehigh counties. The bank that started more than 150 years ago in a tiny borough on the banks of the Susquehanna River, now serves customers through a network of branch locations throughout south-central Pennsylvania.

Ross Buehler Falk & Company

Ross Buehler Falk & Company.

The general perception that accountants are boring number crunchers whose greatest asset to a business is at tax time doesn't hold up at Ross Buehler Falk & Company. While tax preparation is a vital client service, it basically is a necessary and important report on a client's past. Working with clients in attacking the future is where the action is in this firm, which is now one of Lancaster County's largest and most-respected certified public accountant organizations.

Utilizing a team approach, the firm provides solutions to a wide range of challenging financial problems. Its clients include contractors, real estate developers, professionals, and nonprofit organizations, as well as snack food, publishing, service, and manufacturing companies, and companies in a number of other industries. These clients are in 20 states and three foreign nations.

The company's international operations are increasingly important to clients. As the world undergoes dramatic change, management must be aware of how such change will affect business. It must understand the impact of global economic situations. And, if a company wants to participate in the rewards of international ventures, it must first understand the social climate and customs of the nations where it intends to do business.

Obtaining such information and providing it to clients is a specialty at Ross Buehler Falk & Company. The team has successfully aided clients in international financing, mergers, and acquisitions.

The firm was formed in 1985 when six professionals with a variety of accounting specialties set up the business in downtown Lancaster. Today more than 20 employees work in a spacious suburban building on the Lititz Pike. Services provided include auditing, accounting, and tax services; business and financial planning; estate and trust planning; financial management and computer consulting; and mergers, acquisitions, and liquidations.

An important part of the firm's service to clients is its in-house computer expertise. Clients can utilize the firm's extensive knowledge of the latest hardware and software to start or improve their own computer operations.

Providing clients with such "big firm" expertise while maintaining service with a very personal approach has been the key to success for the firm. It keeps abreast of trends and new technology affecting the profession by maintaining memberships in important organizations. In fact, senior partner Jack Ross, who created the talented organization, is one of only four persons outside of Philadelphia or Pittsburgh in the past 40 years to have served as president of the Pennsylvania Institute of Certified Public Accountants.

This commitment to service extends to the Lancaster community as well. The company totally underwrites employee participation in a wide range of community, civic, service, and cultural organizations.

Community Hospital of Lancaster

Community Hospital of Lancaster.

Community Hospital of Lancaster observed its 50th anniversary in 1992, but its roots go back even further. In 1921 a group of wives of Lancaster osteopathic physicians opened a free clinic supported and managed by the Osteopathic Club. From the first, the group had plans for a hospital, but construction delays were brought on by the Great Depression. It was not until June 29, 1942, that the first patients were admitted to Lancaster Osteopathic Hospital.

From that original 35-bed facility has grown a modern teaching hospital with 206 beds, a medical staff of 150 physicians, 1,000 employees, and hundreds of dedicated volunteers. More than 400 physicians have received their training at the hospital, taking advantage of the county's widest range of training programs, including residencies in anesthesiology, general practice, internal medicine, obstetrics/gynecology, pathology, pediatrics, radiology, surgery, and urology.

Community Hospital radiologists Dr. Susann E. Schetter and Dr. John J. Pulich interpret images from the CT scanner.

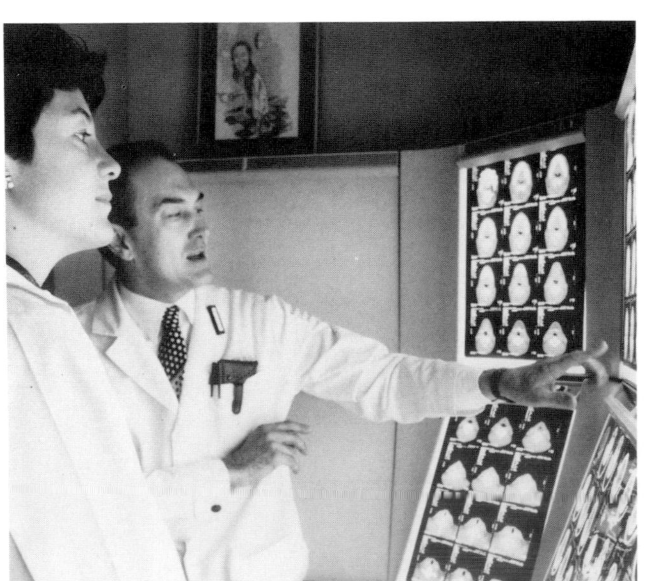

Since its founding, the hospital has pioneered significant medical practices and area health care services. Among these were the county's first renal dialysis unit and Mobile Intensive Care Unit. Community Hospital was also first in the area to offer rehabilitation patient care.

In 1983 the Walnut Street Family Health Center was opened as the hospital's first satellite family practice office. Other hospital outreach projects include Community Counseling of Lancaster, an outpatient mental health facility; the Oxford Medical Center, serving the southern area of the county; and the Heart and Diagnostic Imaging Center, dedicated to the diagnosis, treatment, and prevention of heart disease. In 1991 the Pain Management Institute of Lancaster was opened. Such continued emphasis on community health was reflected in the 1986 name change to Community Hospital of Lancaster.

Community Hospital physicians have consistently been on the cutting edge of medical practice. In 1990 they were first in the county to perform laparoscopic cholecystectomy (gall bladder removal using a laparoscope) and among the first to use laparoscopy and laser surgery to treat urologic conditions.

The hospital serves approximately 8,000 inpatients and 60,000 outpatients annually, and during 1992 donated $11 million in care to the uninsured and underinsured. Its clinics provide low-cost health services to thousands of area residents, and its screening, educational, and wellness programs support the concept of preventive care throughout the community.

Today Community Hospital of Lancaster remains dedicated to treating the whole person in a modern, state-of-the-art, family-oriented health care center. The hospital further aspires to enhance the quality of life throughout the community in partnership with other concerned individuals and organizations. This historical purpose is reaffirmed in the hospital's mission "to provide quality and value in comprehensive and compassionate health care to individuals and families, consistent with the osteopathic philosophy of treating the whole person."

Lancaster General Hospital

Anna McComsey was the first patient admitted to Lancaster's new hospital on December 18, 1893. Like hundreds of the city's 32,000 residents at the time, she had typhoid fever from drinking untreated water. She was discharged as cured 71 days later.

The hospital that treated her was Lancaster General. It came into being when a group led by Rev. Mr. D. Wesley Bicksler, pastor of Salem Evangelical Church, asked influential citizens in Lancaster to consider funding a new hospital, as the other two institutions in the city were frequently filled to capacity.

The response was favorable, and church leaders, merchants, professionals, and other community-minded individuals joined together to help create what today has grown to become a 553-bed, regional, acute-care hospital whose mission has remained much the same as it was 100 years ago.

The goal of the hospital has always revolved around providing the best-quality care for its patients. That has meant constructing buildings and obtaining modern equipment to ensure superior medical care, seeking qualified employees and properly training them for specific tasks, attracting and keeping the best medical and dental staffs, and being a good neighbor to the citizens of Lancaster County.

The hospital has passed numerous milestones as the needs of the community have fostered its growth. There have been major expansions of facilities at its present North Duke Street location. In place today is a residency program that has trained hundreds of physicians over the past 20 years. For more than 90 years the Lancaster General School of Nursing has trained and graduated thousands of nursing professionals who have gone to the aid of the sick and injured.

The hospital's Mid-Atlantic Heart Institute, a regional center for the care of cardiac patients, has gained national recognition for its open-heart program. The hospital also has the only accredited trauma center in Lancaster County.

In addition to a full range of primary care services, Lancaster General also has a neonatal intensive care unit and a renal dialysis unit. Among several outpatient satellite locations is a major facility which, when opened in 1994, will provide a broad range of outpatient services and physician offices.

As a vital contributor to the welfare of the community, Lancaster General has continued in its mission to serve all of Lancaster County. The hospital is committed to responding to the needs of the community through various free programs such as: ChildProtect, an immunization program to protect youngsters from childhood diseases; KidSafe, a leading screening program for children at risk for lead poisoning; HeartBeat CPR training for the community; senior citizen health assessments through the Lancaster County Office of Aging; and valuable community education programs that promote good health.

Through the years, Lancaster General Hospital has been privileged to have had sound management guiding its growth and directing the care it provides. It has also had caring and dedicated employees working alongside thousands of volunteers. Both groups have shown tremendous personal pride in the development of the hospital's health-care services and in the fine reputation the hospital enjoys in the community.

The Landis Mansion on North Lime Street was acquired by Lancaster General Hospital in 1896 as its second location.

The ward approach to placing patients was popular in the early 1900s. Today, patients are placed in semi-private or private rooms.

St. Joseph Hospital

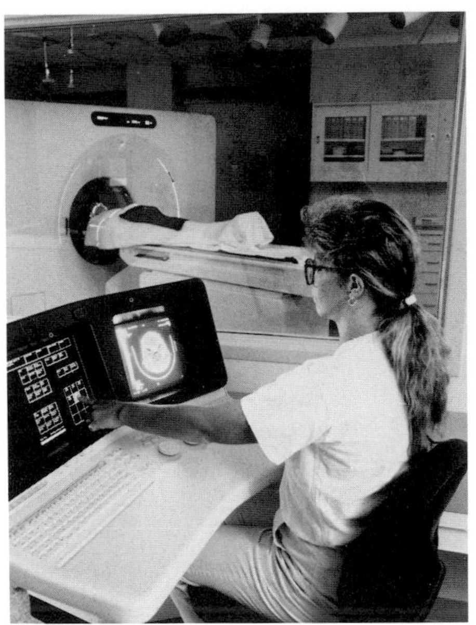

St. Joseph's imaging suite features the latest generation CT scanner.

Lancaster was without a hospital of any kind in 1877, when the Brothers of St. John of God, an order of Papist monks, constructed a building for that purpose at Marietta and College avenues. Dedicated to St. Joseph, it was to be a hospital for men, with a facility for women to follow. But support did not materialize, and the project was abandoned.

The building was purchased in 1883 by the Sisters of St. Francis of Philadelphia. When two sisters from the Glenn Riddle, Pennsylvania, order were sent to Lancaster to prepare the hospital for patients, they found a building without lights, without beds, and without a single water faucet. They were soon joined by four more sisters, a Mother Superior, a pharmacist, a nurse, and a cook. By October of that year, the sisters opened St. Joseph Hospital to patients once again, this time permanently.

In its first year, the hospital treated 121 patients. In 1891 the number had risen to 300 patients, and in 1898, during the Spanish-American War, 169 soldiers were provided medical care. Two years later, a new wing opened in the hospital for the specific care of "operation cases."

Original hospital buildings, some of which were erected in 1877. All have been replaced with modern facilities.

St. Joseph Hospital has always been known for the quality of its nursing. In 1902 the hospital accepted three young women into its first nursing school. Since then, more than 3,000 men and women have graduated from the St. Joseph Hospital School of Nursing.

In 1956 the last portion of the original hospital building was removed to clear the way for a modern facility. Today the 309-bed hospital is dedicated to providing quality, cost-effective health care, innovative programs, and state-of-the-art technology, all within an environment that is consistent with its mission of service to all. In addition to offering traditional medical, surgical, pediatric, psychiatric, and rehabilitative care, St. Joseph is also recognized for such specialty strengths as The Center for Cardiac Care; The Chest Pain Emergency Center; Children's Emergency Services; an accredited community cancer program; and innovative programs for women and children.

St. Joseph Hospital also maintains a 16-bed intensive care/cardiac care unit and a neonatal intensive care unit. The hospital serves as the regional Poison Control Center and also provides a wide range of individual follow-up and home health care services, as well as programs in preventive medicine and health education.

With outpatient services in growing demand, St. Joseph has opened a new two-story addition, The George C. Delp Pavilion, which houses The Day Hospital—a state-of-the-art facility for same-day surgery, chemotherapy, blood transfusions, and laser eye surgery. The building also features 11 new surgical suites, including two dedicated to cardiothoracic surgery.

Three off-site facilities provide convenient, easily accessible outpatient services. St. Joseph Rehab Center-Eden offers physical, occupational, speech, and respiratory therapy, as well as psychological and social services. St. Joseph Cardiac & Rehab Center-Point West, Columbia Avenue, provides non-invasive cardiac diagnostics, physical therapy, and cardiac rehabilitation. The hospital's newest outpatient facility, The WorkConnection, in Lancaster, offers occupational health services to the corporate community.

The Sisters of St. Francis, who labored against great odds to establish Lancaster's first hospital, would surely be pleased if they could see how their work at St. Joseph has grown into a facility with more than 11,000 admissions in 1992.

Corporate Healthcare Strategies, Inc.

Corporate Healthcare Strategies, Inc., does not have a turn-of-the-century history steeped in tradition like so many of the companies it now serves. In contrast, the firm was founded in 1989 to meet a growing demand from corporate management for expertise in developing employee benefits programs.

Corporate Healthcare knows that next to a paycheck itself, nothing is quite so important to an employee as a well-run benefits program. But health-care dollars, in every company, always affect the bottom line, either chipping away at profits or causing the loss of jobs. Corporate Healthcare Strategies exists to help companies meet their employees' needs and at the same time control costs.

Kenneth G. Stoudt, president of Corporate Healthcare Strategies, has spent his entire career developing and administering employee benefits programs. As both a former co-owner and chief executive officer of several companies, Stoudt understands the health-care insurance business both as an employer and as a benefits professional.

David K. Stoudt, executive vice president of the firm, has also dedicated his entire career to the employee benefits arena. Stoudt was an employee benefits manager for a large insurance company and, more recently, president of a third party administration firm. David joined his father as a full partner in early 1991.

Corporate Healthcare Strategies, Inc., has seen the cost of employee benefits skyrocket in recent years and is also aware of the complexity of governmental requirements and the constantly changing needs of the work force. "We can help a company see where it is heading in these areas and provide that company with a blueprint for the future." Ken Stoudt says.

Kenneth G. Stoudt, right, president of Corporate Healthcare Strategies, Inc., and David K. Stoudt, executive vice president.

"We know the benefit marketplace and the needs of companies and their employees, and we are able to bring a degree of independence to the table in our recommendation," David Stoudt explains. As an employee benefits consulting firm, Corporate Healthcare Strategies can help a company see its own strengths and weaknesses and then tailor a unique, affordable program that fits that company's particular needs.

The Stoudts view their company as a problem-solving organization, with the ability to identify with clients and meet their needs. Corporate Healthcare Strategies serves well over 100 companies in the Mid-Atlantic region—with clients in Lancaster, Baltimore, Washington, Philadelphia, and central Pennsylvania—and the Midwest.

Warner-Lambert Company

Lititz native Elmer H. Bobst was president and then chairman of Warner-Lambert through a period of rapid growth and company name changes starting in 1945.

The history of the Warner-Lambert Company has to a large extent run parallel with the advancement of health care from the late 19th century to the present. Founded by pharmacists, the firm has remained committed to its pharmaceutical origins for over 100 years.

Throughout Warner-Lambert's growth into a firm of global importance, a colorful variety of products has been associated with it or with companies that have since come under the Warner-Lambert corporate umbrella. Among the firm's past and present trademarks are names that will not soon be forgotten, such as Smith Brothers, Dentyne, Schick, Chiclets, Hudnut-DuBarry, Cool-Ray, Benadryl, and Listerine.

The story of Jordan Wheat Lambert and the company that bears his name is inextricably intertwined with Listerine antiseptic. Recognized as one of the most successful proprietary products in American marketing history, its modern-day counterpart, Listerine mouthwash, has for many years been produced in the firm's Lititz, Lancaster County plant.

Dr. Joseph Lawrence, in 1879, developed the original formula for Listerine as a safe and effective antiseptic for use in surgical procedures. Ownership of the formula transferred to Lambert, who, in 1881, established the Lambert Pharmacal Company to manufacture and market the product for the medical profession.

Listerine became so popular that in 1914 Lambert made it available for general consumer use. As a result, Americans learned a new word, "halitosis," and Listerine carved out its own special niche as one of the most successful and enduring products in marketing history.

In 1856, well before Listerine was produced commercially, a young drug store owner and pharmacist in Philadelphia developed a method for encasing harsh-tasting medicines in a sugar shell. Thirty years later he gave up the retail shop to concentrate on drug manufacturing under his own name, forming William R. Warner & Co.

In various locations throughout the country at the time, other pharmaceutical and personal-care products were being developed that would one day come together under Warner-Lambert, as it exists today. There was Thomas Adams, of New York City, who in 1869 chanced upon the first chewing gum, when his supply of chicle from Mexico was a failure as a synthetic rubber. Another small business in Detroit was producing botanical medicines in 1866; its principals were Hervey C. Parke and George S. Davis. Products such as Sloan's liniment and Corn Huskers lotion also joined the firm's product line during the first half of this century.

Lititz native Elmer H. Bobst was named president of William R. Warner & Co., in 1945. In 1950 the company went public and changed its name to Warner-Hudnut, Inc.

Under Bobst, the firm acquired Chilcott Laboratories in 1952, a company credited with making the first multivitamin product: Matline with cod-liver oil. Sales soon reached $100 million, and the business merged with the Lambert Company in 1955 to become Warner-Lambert Pharmaceutical Company.

In 1956 the Emerson Drug Company of Baltimore was acquired, with its well-known product line of Bromo-Seltzer. Then, Nepera Chemical Company was added, with its already famous line of Anahist antihistamine products. That same year Bobst, in his added capacity as chairman of the firm, acted on his admiration for the strong work ethic found in Lancaster County and located the newest Warner-Lambert plant in his home town of Lititz. That plant is now the firm's main domestic facility for production of all consumer health products. It also services a variety of businesses for Warner-Lambert.

In the early years, work in the Lititz plant was devoted primarily to the DuBarry line of quality cosmetics and perfumes. During the 1970s and early 1980s, the products being manufactured in Lititz shifted entirely to pharmaceuticals requiring a doctor's prescription. These medications were distributed under the well-known Parke-Davis label.

From the mid-1970s to present, there has been a gradual shift to the manufacturing of consumer health products in the Lititz plant. Products in this extensive line have included Listerine antiseptic mouthwash, Listermint mouthwash, EPT Pregnancy Test Kits, Caladryl Cream and Lotion, Lubriderm lotion and bath oil, Anusol cream ointment and suppositories, and Effergrip denture adhesive.

The Lititz facility is unique within the Warner-Lambert system in that it houses more than one division, and since 1982 it has served as the firm's Mid-Atlantic Distribution Center. The center maintains critical inventories of all Warner-Lambert products—including consumer health, pharmaceutical, and confectionery items. From Lititz, products are shipped to customers throughout the Mid-Atlantic region.

The Distribution Center opened in 1982 and was expanded in 1989, with a second expansion completed in 1992. The total facility size is now in excess of one million square feet of floor space.

The Warner-Lambert plant in Lititz.

The most recent arrival to the Lititz facility has been the Warner-Chilcott Division. Part of the Parke-Davis Pharmaceutical Group, Warner-Chilcott manufactures generic pharmaceuticals—more-economical versions of many widely prescribed drugs already on the market under well-known brand names. This operation started in 1988 and has shown increasing volume annually.

The Lititz facility is a major contributor to the success of the total Warner-Lambert Company. Products manufactured in the Lititz plant in 1991 resulted in over $500 million in sales to the corporation. During that same year, total corporate sales were approximately $4.4 billion.

Warner-Lambert recognizes that success is not possible without dedicated employees. The current work force in the Lititz facility numbers about 900, including all production, maintenance, warehouse, professional, and managerial employees.

As the company looks to the next century, efforts are being made to empower employees and make them partners in the growth

This 1927 ad helped popularize such terms as "halitosis" and memorable slogans such as, "Even your best friends won't tell you."

and success of the firm. Warner-Lambert's stated mission is "...to safely manufacture high-quality products in a cost-effective and timely manner, in accord with, and in the spirit of, our corporate creed." The mission statement refers to the firm's fundamental responsibilities to five major constituencies: customers, employees, shareholders, suppliers, and society in general.

Warner-Lambert practices good corporate citizenship with the donation of products, staff time, and funding in support of worthy organizations in the community. The firm encourages all employees to participate in the annual United Way campaign and has supported Junior Achievement for many years. The firm was recently cited for special honors by Millersville University for support of education for women and minorities.

Lancaster Bible College

One of the early sites of Lancaster School of the Bible.

In the early 1930s, most people were just trying to hold on to what they had. The effects of the Great Depression were as evident in Lancaster as in the rest of the country. But one man had a vision that transcended the financial circumstances of the time. Dr. Henry Heydt felt that students of the Bible needed more than lectures. They needed the opportunity to study and discuss theological subjects, and the ability to read the scriptures in their original language in order to gain a better understanding of the Bible. Heydt resigned from the pastorate of the Lancaster Moravian Church in August 1933 to become the founder and first president of Lancaster School of the Bible, now known as Lancaster Bible College.

No tuition was charged during the first 18 years of the college's existence. There were no appeals for funds. Instead, the faculty divided up what money was dropped in offering boxes at the school. Sometimes, Heydt received three dollars a week or less. He supplemented his income by serving as pastor of the Lancaster Tabernacle, now known as Grace Baptist Church.

The first classroom of Lancaster Bible College was on the second floor of a building at West Orange and Pine streets. The first floor was the showroom of Jones Pontiac. The college moved to 211-213 North Duke Street in the spring of 1934. Five years later it moved into larger quarters at 128-130 North Mulberry Street. A gift in 1957, from J. Martin Esbenshade and his wife, of 15 acres of farmland and buildings along Eden Road marked the the beginning of the present campus of Lancaster Bible College. In 1962 the Ebenshades donated another four-and-a-half acres, and the college purchased 16.5 more to round out today's 36-acre campus.

A two-year curriculum was initially offered by the school. Later it was expanded to three years. The early faculty and administration wanted to concentrate on studying the content of the Bible. Basic general education and some practical ministry courses were also offered.

During the 1960s, many graduates were going on to four-year colleges to earn a degree. A fourth year of studies was added to Lancaster Bible College in 1972, and in 1973 the college was authorized by the Pennsylvania Department of Higher Education to grant a Bachelor of Science degree in Bible. Today L.B.C. continues as a Bible college that is professional in nature and fully accredited.

The administration is now engaged in a period of strategic planning and development that will determine the college's future goals. Dr. Gilbert A. Peterson, president of Lancaster Bible College, says the institution is establishing a graduate program, as well as expanding its professional majors to include fields such as secondary education, management, and communications. In addition, with a number of Bible colleges in the northeast closing in recent years, Lancaster Bible College is exploring the establishment of programs that could serve day or evening students outside of the Lancaster area.

"We are in a positive financial position and are properly accredited. Our enrollment in the fall of 1993 was 507 and growing," says Peterson. "As we advance in this decade, we are still committed to the purpose Dr. Heydt established: teaching the content of the Word of God to effectively prepare people for productive ministries."

Today's academic complex, including classrooms, formal lounge, and media center.

Franklin & Marshall College

The first classes of Franklin College were conducted in 1787, in this downtown Lancaster building known as the "Brew House."

The new nation's leaders made education a high priority in 1787. Only nine colleges existed throughout the 13 colonies at the start of the Revolution, but with the war over, the number of new institutions began growing rapidly.

In Pennsylvania there was concern that a large German population might remain more German than American unless a means of education could be provided to teach them American ideals. A liberal education was also deemed necessary if succeeding generations were to successfully perpetuate the Republic.

Nowhere were these concerns more strongly expressed than in Philadelphia and Lancaster. Thus it was that Franklin College came into existence through the efforts of four clergymen, all graduates of German universities. Classes were first conducted on July 18, 1787.

Benjamin Franklin, with a gift of £200, was the most generous contributor toward the founding of the college named in his honor.

Classes were conducted in a small building on Mifflin Street known as the "Brew House" and at nearby Trinity Lutheran Church. A year later, classes moved to a building on North Queen Street, near James, called the "Store House."

But support for the college waned, and despite a land grant from the Pennsylvania General Assembly of 10,000 acres in northern Pennsylvania, the young institution struggled financially and ceased operation after only two years. In the ensuing decades, the school's trustees continued to exist as a board, and classes were held from time to time in the college buildings. During this period the name of the institution was changed to Franklin Academy.

Not far from Lancaster, in rural Mercersburg, the Reformed Church sponsored the founding of another college, Marshall College, which opened in 1836 with two professors and 18 students. The new college was named for Chief Justice John Marshall, with Frederick Augustus Rauch, a German refugee and one of Europe's most dedicated scholars, as its first president.

The two schools merged in 1853 to become Franklin & Marshall College. Following Marshall's tradition, it was an all-male school. James Buchanan was named president of the first Franklin & Marshall College board of trustees, four years before becoming president of the United States.

The highest point of land

The original buildings on the present-day campus of Franklin & Marshall College were Old Main and the two literary society halls that flank it.

on the west side of Lancaster was selected as the campus of the new college. Here, a stately Gothic structure, known today as Old Main, was erected, flanked by two smaller literary society halls.

During the Civil War, students and alumni fought on both sides, and immediately following the Battle of Gettysburg, Goethean Hall, one of the original literary society buildings, was used as a soldiers' hospital.

A philosophy of liberal education took shape during the period immediately following the war. President John Williamson Nevin believed that liberal education for its own sake must always be the sole reigning objective of the college.

Vocational studies and narrow specialization, Nevin argued, must become secondary goals. His leadership set the tone for the liberal spirit of inquiry which had begun in the great German universities of the day and which, in some form, would always be a part of the Franklin & Marshall tradition.

The importance of science in the curriculum was recognized in 1903 with construction of a science building under the leadership of Dr. John Summers Stahr, an 1867 graduate of the college who remained as a tutor, gradually worked his way up to the presidency, devoted his entire adult life to the college, and is credited with bringing it into the 20th Century.

The college has continued to pursue excellence in science education and has been credited as one of the nation's most highly rated undergraduate institutions for chemistry, geosciences, and pre-medicine. The Martin Library of the Sciences, which opened in 1989, is an outstanding facility and a demonstration of the continuing commitment of the college to this area of study.

While Franklin College included both male and female students in 1787, the institution had not been coeducational since the merger in 1853. That all changed in 1969 when women were once again admitted. Today women make up nearly half of the student body. The college has recognized the growing role of women in society, and in fall 1992 a Women's Center was dedicated on campus.

When most F&M students went off to fight in World War II, college President Theodore "Prexy" Distler convinced the U.S. Navy to establish officer training programs at Franklin & Marshall.

While the present-day college may bear few outward similarities to its predecessors of the last two centuries, it has remained true to the early educational philosophies espoused by such great educators as Frederick Augustus Rauch, John Williamson Nevin, and John Summers Stahr, to name just a few.

The college has in more recent years upgraded the humanities curriculum. Drama has long been among the college's gifts to the community through the Green Room Theatre, and now music is also offered as a major.

U.S. News and World Report lists Franklin & Marshall College as one of the top 35 liberal arts colleges in America. The 1,800 students now enrolled in the college come from 45 states and 48 foreign countries.

Women students were once again admitted to F&M in 1969.

Acorn Press, Inc.

Acorn Press' 13,000-square-foot printing plant at 500 East Oregon Road provides top commercial printing to the Lancaster area.

Acorn Press, Inc., is a good example of a family business that has prospered in Lancaster County's favorable economic environment. Don Roseman, Sr., and Don Roseman, Jr., installed a press in the garage of their home on Pleasure Road in 1956. The printing business was a success, and when the family moved to Valley Road two years later, the press went with them. As business increased, the Rosemans expanded the operation to other buildings on their property, and they incorporated in 1964.

A major turning point in the company's history came in 1974, when Acorn Press secured a loan through the Lancaster Industrial Development Authority. This loan funded construction of a 13,000-square-foot printing plant at 500 East Oregon Road and the purchase of a two-color, 38-inch press. The move helped transform the company from a small job shop to one of the top commercial printing companies in the area.

Staying competitive in the commercial printing industry means keeping up with the latest technology. Acorn Press was one of the first companies in the area to have a Scitex electronic prepress image assembly and color correcting system. The company presently has the latest computerized laser scanning systems and desktop publishing capabilities. The investments in modern technology have paid off, and to accommodate the increased business that keeps its four-, five-, and six-color presses busy, Acorn Press recently expanded its facility for the fourth time; it now occupies over 34,000 square feet.

Hard work and uncompromising quality are at the heart of Acorn Press, and its accomplishments have been recognized with numerous awards over the years. Most recently, the company received five gold and five silver medals in the commercial printing industry's 1991 Neographics Awards.

In addition to its almost 100 regular employees, Acorn Press supports one of Goodwill Industries' job site programs. From 12 to 20 workers are employed at Acorn Press to perform packaging and assembly operations. The company is also well represented in other areas of community service, encouraging its employees who serve in leadership positions on the boards of numerous human service, public service, and civic organizations.

Lancaster Newspapers, Inc.

Lancaster Newspapers, Inc., originated with publication of the weekly *Lancaster Journal* in 1794, making the present-day *Intelligencer Journal* the thirteenth-oldest daily in the United States.

The original paper was printed in an office at Euclid's Heads Tavern, a publishing site since the 1770s and the location of Lancaster Newspapers today. On this site Francis Bailey published a newspaper and almanac. He also printed Thomas Paine's *Crisis No. 4,* as well as the fourth edition of *Common Sense* at this location.

The first *Lancaster Journal* was published and edited by Henry Wilcox and William Hamilton. Unlike today the editors of that early newspaper did not think local news was of enough interest to print. Records show only one exception, when on the Fourth of July in 1794 details of the local celebration were recorded in the paper.

An opposition weekly, the *Intelligencer and Weekly Advertiser,* appeared in 1799. One of that paper's original publishers, William Dickson, differed with Pennsylvania Governor Thomas McKean in 1806 on how to reform the state judiciary. He printed material that led the governor to sue him for libel. Dickson was found guilty and sent to jail in Lancaster, from where he continued to edit his newspaper.

In 1839 the *Intelligencer* and the *Journal* merged under the editorship of John W. Forney to become the *Lancaster Intelligencer Journal.* The paper eventually supported the candidacy of Lancaster lawyer James Buchanan for president of the United States.

The *Intelligencer* became a daily in the midst of the Civil War in 1864. Andrew Jackson Steinman, a Lancaster lawyer, purchased the newspaper in 1866 and was editor and publisher until his death in 1917.

Charles Steinman Foltz was part owner and editor with Andrew Steinman from 1887 to 1921, when Foltz sold his interests to Steinman's sons, James Hale and John F. Steinman, who several years earlier had acquired their father's interest.

The *New Era* first appeared in 1877, founded by John B. Warfel and J.M.W. Geist. They published the *New Era* until 1897, when it was taken over by the founder's son, John G. Warfel, along with B.S. Shindle, Andrew H. Hershey, and James D. Landis. Landis later succeeded Geist as editor.

After being sold and then merged with another Lancaster paper, the *Examiner,* the property was bought by Paul Block, the publisher of a dozen newspapers, in 1923. Block sold the *New Era* to the Steinmans in 1928.

The *Intelligencer* was an afternoon newspaper when it merged with the *News Journal,* a morning edition, and resumed its old name of the *Intelligencer Journal,* starting the morning publication that exists today. The *Lancaster New Era* continued as the town's afternoon paper.

Seeing the need for a Sunday newspaper, the publishers founded the *Sunday News* in 1923. Since that time it has made rapid strides in growth and development as a regional publication.

The *Intelligencer Journal, New Era,* and *Sunday News* are three distinct newspapers. The editorial policy of each remains as disparate as the views of its editors and individual staff members.

Lancaster Newspapers' colorful history, its advocacy of press freedom, and its long service to the Lancaster community are displayed in a self-guided, sidewalk museum in the newspaper production building along the first block of South Queen Street. The exhibit also presents an overall history of worldwide printing.

An early edition of The Lancaster Journal, *which was first published in 1794.*

Steinman and Steinman created and first published The Sunday News *on September 16, 1923.*

SUNDAY NEWS

U.S. Participation In World Court Up To Senate, Says White House Spokesmer

REGISTRATION FIGURES NEAR 1922 RECORD

Martial Law For Entire State Of Oklahoma Proclaimed In K. K. K. Fight

,000 State Guards Ready To Move Upon Command Of Walton

Politics Take New Lease Of Life And Citizens Registe

Tilden Retains U. S. Net Crown, Beating Johnston

John Cope's Food Products, Inc.

The Cope dried corn plant near Rheems, in 1910.

Cope employees gathered for a family photo at the firm's first modern facility in Rheems, Lancaster County, Pennsylvania.

John Cope's grandfather began one of the country's first commercial sweet-corn drying operations near Manheim, Pennsylvania, in 1900. Frozen vegetables were still many years in the future, and the Lancaster County farmer knew he could serve the market for a tasty corn product that local people wanted but didn't always have the time or ability to prepare.

Cope's corn products quickly established a reputation for high quality, and additional food items were added through the years as the business passed to each successive generation of the Cope family.

In 1960, John F. Cope, the third generation of dried sweet corn producers, incorporated the business in partnership with several other local businessmen in the food-processing industry. The corporation enjoyed considerable success for the next two decades until a major fire destroyed the Cope processing plant in 1981. Business, however, did not suffer for too long. A new, modern plant was built that upgraded the dehydration operation and expanded the firm's capability to produce new frozen vegetable lines.

Two years after opening the new plant, dried sweet corn powder was developed as an ingredient for the Japanese soup market. The Cope Company now supplies the soup industry with air-dried foods that include peas, corn, okra, and vegetable powders.

Today, after nearly a century of operation, the fourth-generation Cope family still manages the business and distributes food products throughout the world. With 137 employees, the company offers a line of food products that now includes frozen cut and cob corn, frozen peas, frozen vegetable mixes, dried vegetables, and vegetable powders. These items are packaged under both the Cope label and private customer labels and are sold for retail, food service, and industrial distribution.

The firm's modern processing plant in Rheems, Lancaster County, is computer-controlled and highly automated. Corn, peas, and other vegetables are processed rapidly and at the coolest possible temperatures to capture the "just picked" freshness that has established the Cope reputation for exceptional quality.

It is the stated mission of the Cope Company "to provide dedicated service and consistent quality while expanding existing markets and developing new products or processes, so that we may sustain our growth, respond to the needs of our employees, and meet the demands of a rapidly changing society."

The company acknowledges that its future success will be directly proportional to the extent to which it is able to include all employees in decisions that affect the level of quality and service being provided.

Dutch Gold Honey

For most individuals, a heart attack at the age of 30 would prompt one to listen to a doctor's advice of "slow down and take it easy." But W. Ralph Gamber, founder of Dutch Gold Honey, Inc., is certainly not like most individuals. His perseverance and commitment to his business and his family enabled him to transform a hobby into the largest independent packing operation in the United States.

Following his heart attack, Ralph and his wife, Luella, purchased three hives of bees for $27 at a Lancaster County farm sale in 1946. Beekeeping was meant to be a relaxing hobby for Ralph. That autumn, the Gambers extracted and bottled their first honey crop in their kitchen on State Street.

Hand-written paper labels identified the Gambers' honey as it was sold at local roadside produce stands. Honey sales quickly grew, and soon Ralph was keeping 200 hives of bees but still not producing enough honey to meet customer demand.

So the Gambers' honey-packing operation quickly outgrew the kitchen and moved to the garage, but even that soon proved to be inadequate. In 1953 a new building was constructed across the street to house the expanding business. Cautious about taking such a large step, the Gambers designed the honey-packing plant to look like a house, just in case the honey business did not fulfill their expectations.

In 1957 Gamber and Woodrow Miller, a fellow honey packer from California, decided to design a new honey container to capitalize on the popularity of famous bears such as Winnie the Pooh and Smokey the Bear. Everyone knew that bears loved honey, so what better character to dispense the delicious, golden liquid? Thus the ever popular squeezable honey bear was invented. Years later its popularity continues to grow, and the honey bear container can be found worldwide.

After two expansions of the State Street plant, Dutch Gold Honey was still in need of additional production and warehouse space. The Gambers purchased a 21-acre farm near Rohrerstown in 1974 and built a modern, 40,000-square-foot processing and bottling plant. At that time the company had 11 employees and processed seven million pounds of honey a year.

The company's growth allowed the Gambers' three children to become involved in the business. Bill Gamber is the president of Dutch Gold, and Nancy Gamber is the office manager. Bill's wife, Kitty, is director of advertising. Marianne Gamber runs Gamber Container Inc., which is housed in the same facility. An offshoot of the honey business' need for glass jars, the container company now also distributes various glass and plastic containers to other industries.

Dutch Gold's plant size reached 100,000 square feet by 1991. The number of employees was nearing 45, and the amount of honey processed per year exceeded 30 million pounds. In fact, 12 percent of all the honey packaged in the United States was being shipped from Lancaster, Pennsylvania.

Dutch Gold packages honey in a variety of sizes, from the familiar, one-pound jar to 60-pound pails, 55-gallon drums, and tank trucks. It also offers different flavors of honey, such as orange blossom, alfalfa, wildflower, and clover.

At 82 years old, Ralph Gamber is still working 10 hours a day and enjoying every minute of it. (So much for the doctor's advice.) When asked why he has been so successful, he smiles and reflects on the company's motto, "We only pack the best."

Ralph W. Gamber, founder and chairman of the board of Dutch Gold Honey.

The Dutch Gold Honey Bear Award is presented by the company each year to an individual who has made significant contributions to the beekeeping industry. The bronze bear is a replica of the original honey bear bottle in which Dutch Gold honey was sold.

Kellogg Company

W. K. Kellogg founded the Kellogg Company in 1906.

While working as a business manager of the Battle Creek Sanitarium in Michigan, Will Keith Kellogg spent much of his time developing cereal foods that patients would find nutritious and easy to eat. His brother, Dr. John Kellogg, had been superintendent of the famous sanitarium since 1876.

In 1894 the brothers first discovered that when they ran boiled wheat dough through rollers it produced thin sheets of wheat which could be toasted and ground into meal.

Quite by accident they left some cooked wheat exposed to the air for more than a day. Rather than discard the batch, they ran it through the process anyhow. Instead of a solid sheet of wheat, what came out of the rollers were individual wheat flakes formed from each piece of grain.

In the hours between flaking and cooking, moisture in the wheat had been distributed evenly throughout the batch and through each piece of grain, allowing individual flaking instead of the thin sheet of cereal. The Kellogg brothers were delighted with their discovery, even though they did not immediately realize that a major new food industry had just been born.

Armed with the new process, Dr. Kellogg started the Sanitarium Health Food Company to produce what he and his brother felt were nutritious foods that had an important place in the diet. When a second food venture, the Sanitas Nut Food Company, was combined with the first company in 1899, W. K. Kellogg was named general manager.

Corn flakes were developed by the Kelloggs in 1898. First made with the whole kernel of corn, they spoiled quickly and were not as tasty as wheat flakes. W. K. quickly discovered that by using just the heart, or grit, of the kernel and adding malt, he could produce a crisp, tasty flake. It was the product on which the future Kellogg Company would be built.

W. K. and his brother did not always agree on how, or even if, their food products should be advertised and promoted. So it was not surprising that the brothers went different directions in business. When W. K. started production in 1906 at his Battle Creek Toasted Corn Flake Company, there were 42 cereal companies in the Battle Creek area—more companies than Kellogg had employees at the time.

While most of the other companies stayed with wheat flakes, W. K. exhibited tremendous faith in his new corn flakes. He advertised extensively and soon became the leader among the cereal companies that survived the early competition. From its initial 33 cases of Kellogg's Corn Flakes a day, the new plant's production grew rapidly during the first year to 2,900 cases a day.

Sales success followed a full-page advertisement in *Ladies' Home Journal* and a promotion that gave away four million sample boxes of cereal, each labeled, "The original bears this signature—W. K. Kellogg."

The cereal company's name changed to Kellogg Toasted Corn Flake Company in 1909; the same

The original Kellogg's Toasted Corn Flakes plant in Battle Creek, Michigan.

year more than a million cases of cereal were sold. Other products and marketing innovations followed quickly. A patented Waxtite™package liner appeared in 1914 and delivered flavor and freshness before unknown in the cereal industry. Then came All-Bran™ cereal in 1916, Bran Flakes™ in 1923, and Rice Krispies™ in 1928. The company name changed for the last time in 1922 when it became Kellogg Company.

American doughboys carried Kellogg cereals to European battle fronts in World War I, and after the war Kellogg started exporting cereal throughout the world. By 1924 production plants had been established in Canada and Australia. Kellogg established one of the first home economics departments in a food company in 1923 to provide consumers with recipes and nutrition information.

W. K. Kellogg again demonstrated the tremendous faith he had in his products when he challenged the business downturn of the Great Depression by doubling the advertising budget and reaching new highs in both production and sales during the decade of the 30s.

During World War II Kellogg Company used part of its Battle Creek plant to pack military K-rations. Another important landmark was established in the 40s when the company added nutrients to its cereals to replace those lost in the milling process, thus establishing Kelloggs as a leader in fortification and nutrition labeling in the food industry.

W. K. Kellogg died in 1951 at the age of 91, just as his company's products were being introduced to yet another generation of American children, this time through the medium of television.

The company expanded worldwide during the 60s and 70s, growing to its present size of 23 operations in 18 countries. Kellogg Company today sells nearly $6 billion worth of food products per year in more than 150 countries.

Kellogg's Lancaster plant was built in 1976 in East Hempfield Township. It employs 520 people and is one of seven food-production operations in Kellogg North America.

It has been said that "Kellogg's grew up with the 20th century," and that "20th-century America grew up with Kelloggs," so when this same company produces 44 percent of the world market for ready-to-eat cereal, it could also be said that "the world starts each day with Kellogg cereals."

Kellogg Company salespeople drove vehicles such as this when calling on customers in 1920.

Kellogg's Lancaster plant was built in 1976.

Stauffers of Kissel Hill

When Stauffers of Kissel Hill was founded in 1932, America was mired in the Great Depression, and the Lititz Pike was still known as the Lancaster-Lititz Toll Road. A lot has changed since then, but not the Stauffer belief in offering quality products and services at a fair price. This philosophy and lots of hard work are responsible for the company's popularity among shoppers and its growth during the past 60 years.

Times were tough in the early 1930s when Roy Stauffer and his wife Florence decided to leave Roy's father's fruit farm and start a roadside market on Kissel Hill, just south of Lititz. The couple had 12 children to raise, but there was an abundance of food products available to them fresh from the farm.

The market quickly grew in size and in the scope of products offered. In addition to the roadside stand, Roy, Florence, and the children also took their fruits and vegetables to Roots, Green Dragon, and other county markets.

The Stauffers took their business seriously, searching out the best products, adding new lines, and always insisting on providing customers with excellent service. Trips to Philadelphia and Baltimore produce markets were made with the intent of getting the freshest possible produce not available at local farms.

Profits from the business went back into growth and expansion, always with an eye on ways to increase customer satisfaction.

In the 1950s the suburban housing boom created a temporary marketing problem for the business, which had become known as "Stauffers of Kissel Hill." A development known as "Mayfield" was constructed in the area, and because of prominent signs advertising the development, and new residents' unfamiliarity with local geography, the area began to take on the Mayfield name.

The Stauffers, aware that such a trend wasn't in their best interest, had a sign painted and placed on their building. "This is Kissel Hill," it proclaimed. The old name was retained, and reinforced when a local television station erected a Kissel Hill sign as part of its promotional efforts in the early 1960s.

The growth of suburban housing developments had another effect on the Stauffers, as well. Rows of houses sitting in former farm fields needed landscaping, so the Stauffers increased the volume of trees and shrubs in their market inventory.

Staying alert to trends in the business has helped the Stauffers become industry leaders. In the 1950s the Kissel Hill market, which had grown dramatically from the original roadside stand, installed ramps in place of steps to better serve customers. But the ramps presented another problem. They were a bit steep and shopping carts tended to gain speed on the downward slope of the sales floor. Stauffers was probably the first market in the nation to offer customers shopping carts with hand brakes.

In 1964 the Oregon Pike market was opened to serve customers in this rapidly developing region of the county. Here, too, the lawn and garden interests of homeowners were taken into account in the market's design and operation. Continued suburban growth around Lancaster resulted in the opening of two new markets in 1970, one in Roherstown and the other in Leola.

Stauffers continued to provide its customers with the newest products available and, at the same time, to keep prices competitive. Scanner registers were installed and new refrigeration equipment was added to keep produce fresher. Product offerings were expanded, including adding craft centers to the markets to meet a growing interest in the hobby.

With four locations selling a large volume of landscaping and garden materials, Stauffers decided to invest in its own landscaping company, which opened in Leola in 1978. Garden centers were opened in York and Harrisburg in the 1980s. Trucks bearing the new SKH logo were soon common sights in new housing developments throughout the region.

Tragedy struck in 1986 when a major fire erupted at the Roherstown market. No sooner had the embers cooled, however, than dedicated employees were busy setting up temporary quarters to keep the business going.

It was a good example of employee dedication to the company, and why SKH Management feels company success is due in large part to its employees. Many employees have been with the company for 15 to 20 years. "People working together makes the difference," is more than a motto at Stauffers of Kissel Hill; it is a way of life.

The company adheres to the original Stauffer family philosophy of providing quality products at a fair price with excellent service to customers. This is exemplified by the "Saturday Night Clearance" tradition at SKH markets. The company, refusing to sacrifice its reputation for quality produce, offers bargain prices to shoppers on Saturday night to clear out inventories, so the following week will start off with fresh stocks.

Today, Stauffers of Kissel Hill, with sales exceeding $45 million annually and with 750 employees, is one of the county's top 25 employers. It ranks among the top 50 in the nation's garden center industry and provides a vital outlet for many locally grown farm products.

SKH has come a long way from that first roadside stand at Kissel Hill—but not so far that it can't reach back and touch the roots on which it was founded.

Hammond Pretzel Bakery

Employees of Hammond Pretzel Bakery at the company's West End Avenue home just before World War II.

William Hammond had first made pretzels before the turn of the century. But 40 years passed before he and his grandson, William Lichty, put the family pretzel recipe back to work again in the midst of the Great Depression in 1931.

Both men had lost their jobs, and work was not likely to be found anytime soon. So they constructed a coal-fired hearth oven in a garage at the rear of 716 South West End Avenue in Lancaster and started a hand-rolled pretzel business that continues at the same location to this day.

The only things at all sure about the young pretzel business were the recipe, the know-how, and the readily available labor. But the pretzel bakery made something everyone liked. It soon had two trucks delivering its pretzels to corner grocery stores throughout the county. By the start of World War II, demand for Hammond pretzels kept two shifts of workers busy daily.

The forties proved difficult in the pretzel business. Employees were lost to the war effort, and gasoline was rationed, limiting deliveries to stores. Following the war, the business had to be built up again.

The firm added its first rotary oven in 1946. That same year, a pretzel-twisting machine was invented, but Hammond pretzels continued to be rolled and twisted by hand, as they still are today.

Hammond Pretzels are now being made by the fifth generation of Hammond's descendants. The firm is owned and operated by Tom and Carol Nicklaus, whose son and daughter are also involved in the business. Carol is the daughter of William Lichty, co-founder of the company.

Lancaster County Magazine recently named Hammond's the "Best Pretzel in Lancaster County" for the fourth year in a row. The honor comes as no surprise to the owners, who say the labor-intensive hand-rolling is gentle on the dough and results in a hard, but not bone hard, pretzel that is crisp, flaky, and easy to eat.

Very little advertising has been needed to sell Hammond pretzels. Its makers say the pretzel is the perfect snack for these health-conscious times since it contains almost no fat and no cholesterol, but it does have protein and carbohydrates.

The firm now has 20 employees and does over $1 million worth of business a year. It is one of the last bakeries in the area that hand rolls every pretzel made. About the only concession the bakery has made to modern trends is the use of 100 percent vegetable oil in the baking process in place of lard.

Zimmerman Foods, Inc.

If any good came of the Great Depression, it was an entrepreneurial spirit born of financial necessity. So it was that a New Danville dairy farmer started selling a special cheese his family seemed to make better than anyone else.

Clayton Shenk started commercial production of cup cheese in the basement of his home in 1929. It was sold in Lancaster's southern and central markets to the county's Swiss-German residents already familiar with the American version of "Koch Kase," a soft cheese originally brought to Lancaster County by German immigrant farmers.

Unlike conventional cheese that could be cut in blocks or sliced, this one was soft like a spread and was usually hand-dipped into the customer's own container, thus the name cup cheese.

For nearly 20 years Shenk's cup cheese was made along the New Danville Pike in the basement of the Shenk home. In 1947 production was moved into a modest building next to the farm home and has continued uninterrupted at that location to this day.

The business was purchased from the Shenk family in 1988 by William E. Zimmerman, who had been seeking a food business with unlimited potential. The company was renamed Zimmerman Foods, Inc., but retained the familiar Shenk trademark on the packaging of both cup cheese and a growing line of mustards, relishes, jams, jellies, and fruit spreads. It has prospered under Zimmerman's hands-on management, as he has expanded the product line and sought new markets for existing items.

Cup cheese remains the company's single largest product. Because it is almost totally free of fat or cholesterol, it has caught the attention of a diet-conscious industry. Cheese-lovers who taste Shenk's Cup Cheese often compare it to brie—and are pleasantly surprised to discover its nutritional advantages over the better-known cheese.

Shenk's has long been known for its green tomato relish. Now a line of dipping mustards has taken over second place in the product line as hard pretzels continue to grow in popularity.

Zimmerman's "Pennsylvania Dutch Gourmet Foods" also include fruit products, such as dandelion jellies and mission-fig jams, along with gooseberry, nectarine, peach, raspberry-rhubarb, and many more natural, fruit-flavored specialties.

Peach-pecan and blueberry-walnut jams are but two of the delicious spreads that double as dessert toppings. There are also fruit butters, no-sugar-added fruit spread, and specialty condiments, such as sweet-pickled watermelon rind, chow-chow, and stuffed peppers.

Zimmerman Foods, Inc., offers great-tasting examples of traditional Pennsylvania Dutch products that have found a welcome niche in a contemporary gourmet foods market. Just as they have been for more than 60 years, the products that carry the Shenk label are still prepared in the careful, hands-on manner that first made them so popular such a long time ago.

Photograph of the C. H. Shenk cheese (predecessor to Shenk Cheese Co. and Zimmerman Foods, Inc.) stand at Lancaster Southern Market circa 1954. Shenk's cup cheese is still sold at Lancaster Central Market.

Turkey Hill Dairy

The Turkey Hill Dairy processing plant in 1940.

Dairy farmer Armor P. Frey put bottles of fresh milk on ice in the back of his touring sedan in 1931 and sold the milk door to door near his farm along the Susquehanna River at Washington Boro. It was the start of Turkey Hill Dairy.

Frey's small dairy enterprise soon included his three sons, Glenn, Charles, and Emerson. The boys were each paid two dollars a week and provided with a car. Their responsibilities included farm field work and milking cows, as well as bottling, selling, and delivering the dairy's milk, and even collecting bills. It was a grueling daily schedule—customers wanted their milk delivered before breakfast, and with so many other dairy farmers selling milk in the same way, competition was fierce.

By the time the boys bought the dairy business from their father in 1947, two delivery routes had been established, one going north to Columbia, and the other south to Safe Harbor. The older Frey continued to manage the farm and sell his milk to his sons, who ran the dairy. The farm remains in the Frey family to this day.

The cow barn and processing plant at Turkey Hill Dairy in the early 1950s.

Glenn, Charles, and Emerson understood that hard work and sacrifice would be necessary to make the dairy successful. They agreed to pay themselves just $25 a week and their employees $100 a week. Unusual as the arrangement was, it launched the Freys on a lifelong commitment to their workers, and it brought a recognition of just how important employees were to the success of the dairy. To this day the Freys have never ceased to believe that people are the key to success.

They also practiced good-old Lancaster County frugality in their business. Equipment was not replaced simply because an improved model came along, and old buildings usually underwent reconstruction instead of being torn down. In fact, a portion of the dairy's original refrigerator room can still be found in the present plant.

The Frey brothers, like their father, followed business principles that grew out of their strong religious background. They viewed themselves as stewards of resources that had been entrusted to them. So it was not surprising that the young owners of the dairy soon counted community service and charitable contributions among the more enjoyable fruits of the company's success.

In those earlier days, before cholesterol became a health concern, dairy products were valued for their high butterfat content, known to customers as cream. Milk quality was determined by the amount of cream that rose to the top of the bottle. Dairies gained or lost customers by a difference of a fraction of an inch of cream in their milk.

Armor Frey always believed in delivering a high-quality product at a fair price, and when it was cream his customers wanted, he found the cows to produce it; he blended the high-cream milk from Jersey and Guernsey cows with that of the dominant and high-producing Holsteins. Whatever the measure of quality through the years, Turkey Hill dairy products have always been rated among the best. But quality alone was not sufficient to carry the dairy through the 1950s and 1960s, when the emergence of supermarkets resulted in a drop in home-delivery customers.

While other small dairies struggled or went out of business, Turkey Hill fought back by expanding its home-delivery line to include soda, bread, soup, and ice cream. Other dairy farmers laughed at the move, but it wasn't long before Frey's had bought out at least a dozen of its struggling competitors, including the Queen and Moore dairies in Lancaster.

Turkey Hill persevered with home-delivery milk routes long after other dairies had given up on the very service that had gotten them into business. That era, however, became history when the last home delivery route ended on February 10, 1992.

Ice cream became available along with Turkey Hill milk products in the 1950s. It was first made by the Freys in a five-gallon, hand-cranked freezer. The dairy made ice cream on Mondays, Wednesdays, and Fridays, then loaned out the freezer to customers on other days.

In 1980 a large expansion of the ice cream plant set the stage for a major launch of Turkey Hill Premium Ice Cream into Philadelphia. By 1992 Turkey Hill was selling more than 25 million half-gallons of ice cream, all produced at the dairy, in one of the most modern ice cream plants in the country.

Another innovation that spurred the growth of Turkey Hill Dairy for many years was its decision in 1967 to establish its own retail outlets. The steady growth of Turkey Hill Minit Markets helped make Turkey Hill ice cream and other dairy products a favorite brand throughout the Middle Atlantic states.

In recent years Turkey Hill has responded to the needs of weight watchers and cholesterol counters with the introduction of such popular products as diet iced tea, frozen yogurt, and Gourmet Lite ice milk. Nonfat frozen yogurt and orange-, lemon-, and cherry-flavored tea coolers have also been developed by Turkey Hill to meet the changing tastes and diets of its customers.

In just the past 10 years, Turkey Hill has doubled its fluid milk and drink sales from 18 to 36 million quarts a year. During that same period ice cream sales have increased 10-and-one-half times.

Now also sold in supermarket chains outside the Lancaster area, Turkey Hill ice cream is today available from Connecticut to Virginia, making it one of the top-selling brands in the country.

In addition to a taste the public loves, Turkey Hill ice cream can also attribute its acceptance to the large variety of flavors available. The dairy produces 49 flavors of ice cream, plus other frozen dessert lines. Tempting flavors such as Chocolate Cherry Cordial, Brownie Nut Fudge, Caramel Cashew Crunch, and Mint Cookies 'N Cream draw devoted customers to Turkey Hill frozen desserts.

When Charles Frey, the youngest of Armor's sons, retired from the business in 1991, he reflected on the growth of Turkey Hill Dairy, saying, "If it was good for the company, we kept it. But when it was time to change and move on, we did that too." It's a modest philosophy that has worked exceptionally well in the family-run business, for the Freys seemed to have had that special intuition needed to know just what to keep and when to move on.

Quintin and Michael Frey, sons of Emerson and Charles, respectively, represent the third generation of the Frey family at the dairy. Today they manage the business for the Dillon Companies of Hutchinson, Kansas, which have owned Turkey Hill Dairy since 1985. It is their desire that the family atmosphere and quality products that have fostered success in the business for so long continue to guide its future growth.

The number of trucks at the Turkey Hill Dairy processing plant today indicates how much the business has grown.

Family members involved in the management of Turkey Hill Dairy are, from left, Charles Frey, Mike Frey, Quintin Frey, and Emerson Frey.

Wilbur Chocolate Company

Whether you bite into a chocolate chip cookie, scoop up some chocolate ice cream, or select a piece from a box of assorted chocolates, part of what you are tasting may have been produced by the Wilbur Chocolate Company of Lititz. In its facilities in Lititz and Mount Joy, Wilbur manufactures chocolate- and confectionery-based products that are incorporated into other confectionery and food items such as candy bars, cookies, and frozen desserts.

Although Wilbur uses modern, computer-controlled processing equipment, the basic procedure for making chocolate remains unchanged from the way the Aztecs prepared "chocolatl" for the Spanish explorers in the 16th century. It starts with the cacao tree, which only grows within a band that stretches between 20 degrees north and south of the equator. The fruit of the cacao tree appears as pods on the trunk and main branches. Because the growing conditions remain nearly constant in the tropics, the pods can be harvested 10 or 11 months of the year.

The pods are opened immediately after harvesting, and the cream-colored beans inside them are removed and allowed to ferment for several days. During this time several chemical changes naturally occur in the beans. These changes result in chocolate's familiar flavor and aroma and give the beans their rich, chocolate-brown color. After fermenting, the beans are dried in the sun or with hot air.

The cocoa beans arrive at the Wilbur processing plant on railroad freight cars or trucks, in sacks weighing up to 200 pounds. The beans are cracked open in a machine called a winnower, and the nibs are separated from the shells. The nibs go to the roasters, where the full chocolate flavor is developed. After roasting, the nibs are ground up until they turn into a liquid, called chocolate liquor. This is the basic material from which all other chocolate products are made.

Pressing this chocolate liquor in a hydraulic press squeezes out cocoa butter, leaving behind a cake of dry cocoa that is ground into cocoa powder for baking or for flavoring chocolate milk. The extracted cocoa butter is added to other chocolate liquor, along with milk and sugar, to make the familiar milk chocolate candy.

Not all chocolate tastes the same or has the same texture. Flavor is determined by the variety of cacao tree, the part of the world where it was grown, and the roasting time and method. Texture is determined by the fineness to which the ingredients of the chocolate are crushed or refined. Because Wilbur makes chocolate products for many customers who have different requirements, its plants have a variety of machines to roast, refine, and "conch" or mix the various products. Once a product has been made to a customer's flavor and texture specification, it is molded into a chip, block, or chunk, or is shipped in a liquid tank truck.

The coating for an ice cram bar has a different flavor and texture than the coating of a candy bar, and that coating is different from the one covering a fruit or nut. Wilbur works with customers to determine just the right chocolate for their final product. The company develops new formulas each week as manufacturers come to Wilbur for the chocolate coating or ingredient that they believe will make their new products most pleasing to you, the consumer.

Groff's Farm Restaurant

Betty Groff was looking for a part-time job in 1960 when the proprietor of a local motel and restaurant asked if she would serve a home-cooked dinner to a bus load of his guests. It was not an overwhelming task for the young Mennonite farm wife and mother. So she served dinner in her home that summer day for 42 IRS employees from Washington, D.C., and in so doing, she created a farm restaurant that would become known world-wide for serving the best in Pennsylvania Dutch cooking.

For a few years Betty Groff's dinners were limited to occasional groups on weekends, but word-of-mouth was working its magic. At one meal in 1965, a particularly curious guest seemed to be asking all the right questions and even followed Betty into her kitchen for a photograph. A month later, Betty and her husband, Abe, were on vacation, when they saw their farm restaurant featured on a full page of the *New York Times.* Their curious guest had been Craig Clairborne, food editor of the *Times.*

They returned home from vacation the same day to find the telephone ringing non-stop, as reservations poured in from all over the country.

A month after the *Times* article, the *Washington Post* also asked to do a story, only they wanted Betty to provide them with another original chicken recipe. She obliged with her own Pennsylvania Dutch creation; named after an Amish contractor, Chicken Stoltzfus is the favorite dish at the farm to this day.

The restaurant has changed very little in 35 years. More than 25,000 dinner guests are welcomed each year to the 1756 stone farmhouse. Vegetables are still home-grown fresh, the ham naturally cured, the prime rib is still aged, and the appetizers at each dinner are still chocolate cake, hearty soups, fresh fruit, and relishes.

Cameron Estate Inn. Photo by Richard Allen

For Betty and Abe, however, change has been inevitable. Abe turned the farm over to others in 1977 and became a full-time partner with his wife in the business. Betty has authored five Pennsylvania Dutch cookbooks and is a popular public speaker. The Groff's son, Charlie, a graduate of the Culinary Institute of America, is manager and executive chef, and together with his wife, Cindy, is continuing the Groff tradition of hospitality, family style.

A few miles away, the Groff's operate the Cameron Estate Country Inn and Restaurant. Here, in one of the great historic homes of Pennsylvania, guests may relax in the fashion of a grand manor while enjoying award-winning continental cuisine. Taking guests back in time, the 1805 Cameron Estate has 18 guest rooms furnished to reflect its Federal heritage, including spacious baronial suites, four-poster beds, and working fireplaces in many rooms.

As the world beats a path to their dining room door, Abe and Betty seem to enjoy their work as hosts to thousands. Their next step is the Groff Farm Golf Club, a public golf course now being carved out of farm land surrounding the restaurant. It is expected to open in late 1994.

Looking back on her unplanned, but eventful career, Betty Groff laughs and sums it up, saying, "It takes a lot of hard work to make it look easy."

Groff's Farm Restaurant and Golf Club, Inc. Photo by Richard Allen

Hotel Brunswick

The former Hotel Brunswick, Queen and Chestnut streets.

The Hotel Brunswick and the United States of America both had their beginnings in 1776. While we all know the story of our nation's creation, few are familiar with the history of the Hofnagle Hotel, a sturdy two-and-a-half-story stone building that served as one of Lancaster's leading hostelries for 84 years. During its lifetime, the structure on the southeast corner of Queen and Chestnut streets was also known as the North American, the American, and the Sheaf of Wheat hotels.

With the coming of the railroad to Lancaster in the 1830s, the hotel site, across from the old train station at Queen and Chestnut streets, was ideal for rail travelers. The office for the first commercial telegraph line in the United States, which ran between Lancaster and Harrisburg, was located in the American Hotel.

Replaced by a three-story structure in 1860, the new hotel took on the name of its next owners, first as the Caldwell House and later the Heister House. It was from the balcony of the Heister House that Abraham Lincoln addressed the citizens of Lancaster during a stop on his trip from Springfield, Illinois, to Washington, D.C., for his first inauguration.

Lincoln was replacing Lancaster's most honored citizen, James Buchanan, in the White House. Soon after Lincoln's appearance here, Buchanan returned to Lancaster, where the hotel was the scene of a great gathering to welcome home the city's favorite son. Within weeks, however, these joyous celebrations gave way to more serious gatherings.

The Civil War became the subject of many meetings and rallies at the hotel. The young men of Lancaster rushed to sign up for the volunteer units being formed in the city. Citizens crowded on the hotel's steps and balcony to wave good-bye to troops boarding trains en route to camps at Harrisburg and Philadelphia. Messages flowed through the telegraph office, and citizens gathered at the hotel to read battle reports and to review the lists of dead and wounded following major battles.

In July 1863 the women of Lancaster, hearing of the great battle at Gettysburg, formed a group to go to the battlefield to aid the wounded. The "Patriotic Daughters" gathered at the hotel to prepare for the railroad trip. The burning of the railroad bridge in Columbia delayed them briefly, but many Lancaster women spent several weeks at Gettysburg performing missions of mercy.

In 1867 the hotel was jammed with firemen from across the state who were in town to participate in what local newspapers described as the "greatest event of its kind ever held in Pennsylvania outside of Philadelphia." It was the first of many such events where the hotel would serve as headquarters for thousands of visiting firemen.

For the next two decades a number of new owners operated the hotel, and famous visitors to the city signed the guest register. Horace Greeley, presidential nominee for the Democrats and Liberal Republicans in 1872, addressed a local gathering at the hotel. In 1880 General Winfield S. Hancock was ratified as the Democratic presidential nominee by a large gathering of supporters.

In 1895 Lily Eshleman Bates purchased the property and renamed it the Imperial Hotel. Former President Theodore Roosevelt stopped by in 1912 and spoke to an enthusiastic Lancaster gathering outside the Imperial. Two years later the site was once again cleared to make room for a newer and larger hotel.

The original Hotel Brunswick was built in 1914. It soon became the center of downtown Lancaster activity and continued to provide high-quality services to a wide range of guests for the next half-century. In 1966 the Brunswick, along with its historic neighbors, met with the wrecker's ball. Progress, in the form of downtown redevelopment, called for a more modern hotel structure.

The Hilton Inn soon rose on the historic site and operated under that name until 1976, when the hotel again became known as the Hotel Brunswick. Guests during this period included President George Bush, actor Harrison Ford, and television personality Ted Koppel.

Now owned by Indepro Group, the Hotel Brunswick is operated by Elmhurst Hospitality, a professional hotel management company with headquarters in Pittsburgh.

In 1991 a major renovation of the hotel took place, including the opening of a state-of-the-art conference center that now hosts a wide variety of business, industry, and government meetings and training programs. The hotel's main lobby has been given a facelift, and many improvements have been made to the 225 guest rooms and suites.

Today the Hotel Brunswick is alive with activities that add much to the life of downtown Lancaster. There are two restaurants, a nightclub and lounge, a sky-lit indoor pool, and a fitness center. The hotel offers room service, remote-control cable television, and more than 30 meeting and banquet rooms of varying size, including the elegant Grand Ballroom with its crystal chandeliers.

The new Hotel Brunswick, at the site of so much of Lancaster's proud history, is a fitting reminder of the way the city has adapted to a changing world, all the while retaining an important part of its colorful past.

Eden Resort Inn

Guests can take a dip in the Eden's indoor/outdoor pools, whirlpool spa, and Finnish sauna.

News was breaking fast and furious in 1972 as Hurricane Agnes flooded Lancaster County and devastated the entire Northeast. Watergate was becoming a household word, and President Nixon won reelection in a landslide. In that same year of dramatic headlines, a major resort inn opened just north of Lancaster, offering the area a new concept in guest services and comfort.

The Treadway Resort Inn, original name of the present Eden Resort Inn and Conference Center, opened with 170 guest rooms and immediately became one of the area's largest and most unique hotels.

A resort inn so close to the city was the brainchild of businessman Drew Antone, who was convinced he could create an inn that would make guests feel more at home by providing unprecedented services and numerous options for activities. He was also convinced that a properly managed inn could successfully serve the away-from-home needs of both the business person and the more casual traveler on vacation. In short, he wanted his inn to be a fun and exciting place for all of its guests.

Garfield's, the family food and fun place.

The Treadway Inn was a success from opening day, and just six years later, a major addition of 65 rooms gave the inn a total of 235 guest rooms. Banquet facilities were also added at the time, and together with its fine restaurant, the inn became a popular meeting place for both travelers and local people looking for a pleasant night out.

With one restaurant, Arthur's, already providing a quiet, more formal atmosphere, the inn opened its second restaurant, Garfield's, in 1983. Garfield's continues today as it was begun, a casual, fun, food place where the decor is as bright as the conversation that unfolds there.

Then came a major expansion in 1988, as the name was

changed to The Eden Resort Inn and Conference Center, and 40 club suites for residential lodgings were added. The club suites, located in detached house-like buildings, provide residential accommodations for persons who have a need to stay long-term—such as people on temporary work assignments or those who are being relocated to the Lancaster area and do not yet have permanent housing.

The club suites each include a full kitchen, dining room, living room, wood-burning fireplace, and remote-controlled color television. Some of the units also have private Jacuzzis.

Among the unique services and facilities at the Eden Resort is a beautiful, tropically landscaped atrium courtyard—the setting for special banquets, elegant wedding receptions, and a fabulous Sunday brunch. The champagne brunch includes omelettes, waffles, crepes, hot entrees, salad bar and fresh fruits, cheeses and breads, and a large selection of desserts. A mime and a strolling clown add a touch of laughter for the entire family. Up to 450 people can be served at one time in the courtyard.

The State Room is a tiered, high-tech training room, soundproof and containing the latest audio-visual equipment. Here business groups conduct highly specialized, intense training for up to 40 persons at one time. More conventional meeting rooms are also available, with personalized services to make any gathering enjoyable and successful.

But even when the business day is over, there is still much to do at the Eden Resort. Those looking for a physical workout have their choice of a fully equipped fitness room, indoor and outdoor pools, tennis, basketball, and shuffleboard. A workout can be followed by a whirlpool spa or a Finnish sauna.

On the more sedate side, the inn has the Video Box game room, first-run in-room movies, and Dionne's Gifts, a shop featuring gourmet edibles and unusual gift items.

Not only does the Eden Resort have its two top-of-the-line restaurants, Arthur's and Garfield's, it also offers guests the Encore Lounge, where sparkling live entertainment can be enjoyed six nights a week. Entertainment may include dancing, light jazz, top 40 music, or comedy.

The Eden Resort Inn has established a strong reputation in the Lancaster area as a host that knows how to make the traveler comfortable. But it is also the gathering place for local folks who appreciate fine food and entertainment. It is not unusual for guests at the inn to find themselves in the company of, say, a famous athlete, for the inn has been home to the Philadelphia 76ers training camp each fall. Other groups also lend a festive atmosphere to the resort as they display their antique cars, campers, or even llamas in the outdoor areas of the resort grounds.

The Eden Resort Inn was established with the vision of complete guest service and comfort. That vision has become a tradition as the inn enters its third decade of providing a home away from home.

Above: From the moment guests step into the Eden's beautiful lobby, they know they have made the right choice.

Below: Eden's lush, tropical, landscaped atrium courtyard... the perfect setting for special banquets, wedding receptions, and a fabulous Sunday brunch.

Bulova Technologies, Inc.

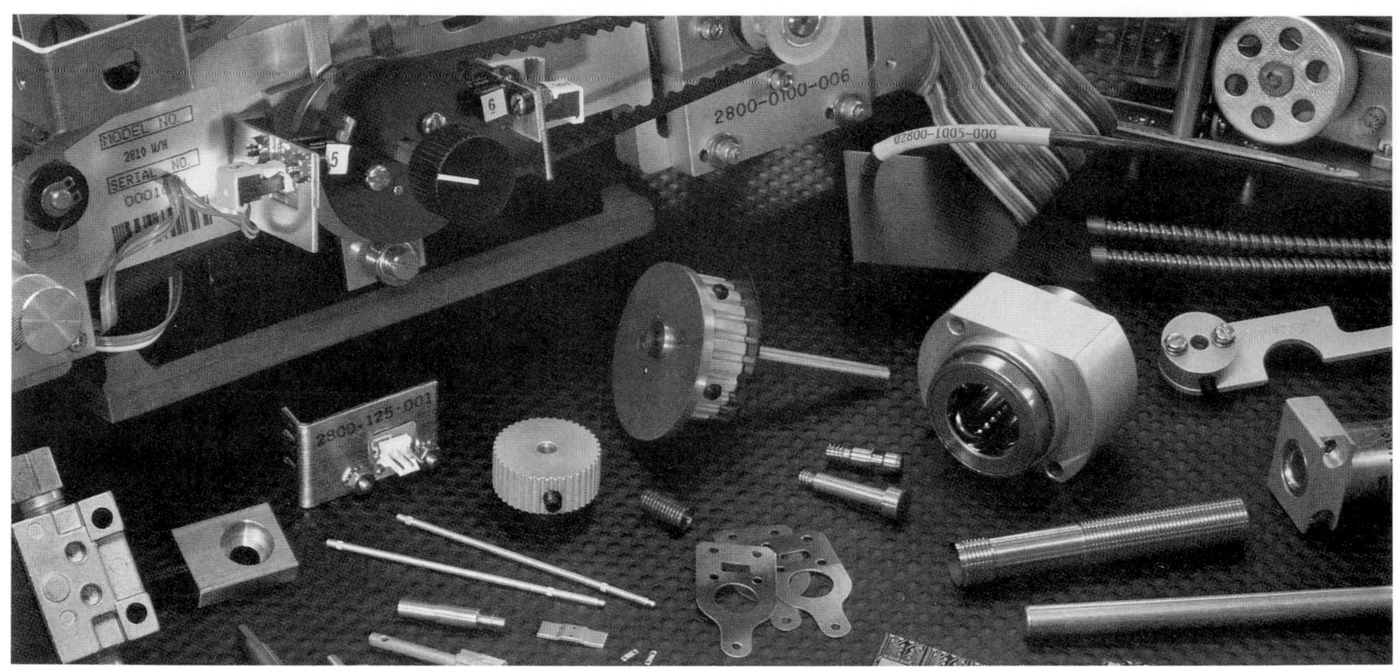

Ultra-precision-machined components and value-added assemblies.

Bulova Technologies, Inc., or BTI, is a relative newcomer to the Lancaster area. Bulova Technologies, a wholly owned subsidiary of the Bulova Watch Company, was established in January 1991 as the result of the merger of Hamilton Technology and Bulova Systems and Instruments Corporation. While BTI is relatively new, both Hamilton and Bulova trace their roots back to the late 1800s and have long-term Lancaster connections.

The idea of watchmaking was first brought to the Lancaster area in 1874 by Messrs. Adams and Perry. After several reorganizations, in 1892 their business was chartered as the Hamilton Watch Company. The company was named in honor of Andrew Hamilton, who owned the land on which the city of Lancaster was built. Hamilton Watch very quickly became recognized as a manufacturer of fine timepieces for the sprawling network of railroads winding across the country.

The Bulova Watch Company was founded in 1875 in New York City by Joseph Bulova. Bulova Watch was originally a merchandising company, importing movements and components, pairing them with Bulova cases and bracelets, and selling them under the Bulova name. Like Hamilton, Bulova also grew rapidly, with an expansion plan based on a strong sales force, national advertising, widespread support of retail jewelers, and delivery of a quality product that was moderately priced. By the early 1900s Bulova became the leading distributor of watches in the United States.

During World War I, both companies supported the U.S. military, primarily by supplying watches and other timepieces to the Army and Navy.

World War II lead to the formation of both Hamilton Technology and Bulova Systems and Instrument Corporation, as once again, both watch companies heeded the call to arms and attempted to support the U.S. military initiative. However, with this war the technology requirements of the armed forces grew beyond watches and timepieces to include marine chronometers, time fuses, and safety and arming devices.

From the late 1940s until

their recent merger, both companies competed with each other in the design and development of fuses, safety and arming devices, and other precision ordnance devices for the U.S. government, prime contractors, and foreign governments throughout the free world.

In 1981 Hamilton Technology, Inc., moved into the building at 101 North Queen Street that still serves as the company's headquarters. Shortly after the merger, BTI closed down its New York operations, relocating the business to the Lancaster area. In addition to its Queen Street operations, the company operates a manufacturing facility at 1000 Stony Battery Road in Hempfield Township.

Today, BTI's primary products are precision mechanical and electronic fuses, triggering devices, and safety and armament devices. These products are used in many of the most sophisticated missiles, tank cannons, and advanced artillery systems utilized by the U.S. military and many of its allies. Bulova products can be found in the weapons systems of F-14, F-16, and F-18 fighter planes; the Apache helicopter; and the M-1 tank. Most recently a number of Bulova products were successfully employed by the allied forces during Operation Desert Storm.

With the recent reduction in defense spending, BTI has been attempting to diversify and utilize its design and engineering expertise and manufacturing capabilities in the production of commercial products. Long-term management would like to see a balance between commercial and defense-related activities. To date, inroads have been made in areas of contract manufacturing for wire bonding and postal equipment, and medical and surgical instruments.

BTI's current vision is to be a world-class manufacturing organization with a focus on engineering, precision machining, and assembly processing. To this end, Bulova is committed to customer satisfaction, teamwork, quality, and continuous improvement.

Samples of fuses and safety and arming devices.

Appendix

Population of Lancaster County

Year	Population
1729	3,500*
1738	12,800*
1752	19,885*
1764	28,000*
1774	35,493*
1785	35,750*
1790	36,147
1800	43,403
1810	53,927
1820	68,336
1830	76,588
1840	84,203
1850	98,944
1860	115,393
1870	121,340
1880	139,447
1890	149,095
1900	159,241
1910	167,029
1920	173,797
1930	196,882
1940	212,504
1950	234,717
1960	278,359
1970	320,079
1980	362,346
1990	422,822

*Estimated from lists of taxables. Other figures from United States Census Bureau.

U.S. Congressional Representation

The Continental Congress

George Ross 1774–1777
Samuel John Atlee 1778–1782
Joseph Montgomery 1780–1782
Edward Hand 1784–1785
Federalist
William Henry 1784–1786
Federalist

The Federalist Period

Frederick A. C.
Muhlenberg 1779–1800
Constitutionalist
John W. Kittera 1791–1801
Federalist
Thomas Boude 1801–1803
Federalist

The Democratic Era

John Whitehill 1803–1807
Anti-Federalist, Republican*
Robert Jenkins 1807–1811
Federalist
Joseph LeFevre 1811–1813
Republican
James Whitehill 1813–1815
Federalist
Amos Slaymaker 1813–1815
Federalist
John Whiteside 1815–1818
Republican*
John Hibshman 1819–1921
Jeffersonian Democrat
James Buchanan 1821–1831
Federalist, Conservative Democrat

The Whig Era

William Hiester 1831–1837
Anti-Masonic
Edward Davies 1837–1841
Whig
Jeremiah Brown, Jr. 1841–1845
Whig
John Strohm 1845–1849
Anti-Masonic, Whig
Thaddeus Stevens 1849–1853
Whig
Isaac Hiester 1853–1855
Conservative Whig
Anthony E. Roberts 1855–1859
American Whig

19th-Century Republicans

Thaddeus Stevens 1859–1868
Republican
Oliver Jesse Dickey 1868–1873
Republican
Abraham Herr Smith 1873–1885
Republican
John Andrew Hiestand ... 1885–1889
Republican
Marriott Brosius 1889–1901
Republican

20th-Century Republicans

H. Burd Cassel 1901–1909
Republican
William Walton Griest ... 1909–1929
Republican
John Roland Kinzer 1929–1947
Republican
Paul Bartram Dague 1947–1967
Republican
Edwin Duing Eshleman . 1967–1977
Republican
Robert Smith Walker 1977–
Conservative Republican

*The Republican party of the early Federal Period was the party of Thomas Jefferson, which advocated states' rights and generally opposed the Constitution of the United States. Later the Republican party split into factions. The Democratic Republicans were the more radical and evolved into the Democratic party. Jeffersonian Republicans were more conservative; many drifted into the National Republican party, which evolved into the Whig party. The present-day Republican party dates from 1854.

Mayors of the City of Lancaster

Elected by the common and select councils

John Passmore 1818–1820
Jeffersonian Republican
Samuel Carpenter 1821–1823
Jeffersonian Republican
Nathaniel Lightner 1824–1830
Jacksonian Democrat
John Mathiot 1831–1843
Whig-supported Masonic Democrat

Elected by the voters

Michael Carpenter 1843–1851
Loco Foco Democrat
Christian Keiffer 1852–1854
Whig-American Party
Jacob Albright 1855
Whig-American Party
John Zimmerman 1856–1857
Democrat
Thomas Burrowes 1858
Anti Slavery Whig
George Sanderson 1859–1869
Democrat

William Augustus Atlee 1869–1871
Republican
Frederick Pyfer 1871–1873
Democrat
William D. Stauffer 1873–1877
Republican
John T. MacGonigle 1877–1884
Democrat
David P. Rosenmiller 1884–1886
Republican
William A. Morton 1886–1888
Democrat
Edward Edgerley.............. 1888–1890
Republican
Robert Clark 1890–1894
Democrat
Edwin S. Smeltz............... 1894–1898
Republican
Simon Shissler 1898–1900
Democrat
Henry E. Muhlenberg..... 1900–1902
Republican
Chester W. Cummings... 1902–1906
Republican
John Piersol McCaskey... 1906–1910
Republican
Frank B. McClain 1910–1915
Republican
Harry L. Trout 1915–1920
Republican
Horace E. Kennedy.......... 1920–1922
Republican
Frank C. Musser 1922–1930
Coalition (Democrat, Independent Republicans)
T. Warren Metzger 1930–1934
Republican
James A. Ross 1934–1938
Democrat
Dr. Dale Cary................... 1938–1950
Republican
Kendig C. Bare/
Howard Bare 1950–1958
Republicans
Thomas J. Monaghan 1958–1962
Democrat
George B. Coe.................. 1962–1966
Republican
Thomas J. Monaghan 1966–1974
Democrat
Richard M. Scott 1974–1979*
Republican
Albert Wohlsen 1979
Republican
Arthur Morris................... 1980–1990
Republican
Janice Stork................................ 1990–
Democrat

*Resigned to become Pennsylvania Adjutant General

Charcoal Iron Furnaces and Forges

Charcoal iron furnaces and forges had colorful names:

Conowingo Creek:
Conowingo Rolling and Slitting Mill

Hammer Creek:
Lower Hopewell Forge, Speedwell Forge, Upper Hopewell Forge

Octorara Creek:
Buckley Forge, Duquesne Forge, Kurtz Bloomery Forge, Middle Sadsbury Forge, Pine Grove Forge, Ringwood Forge, Upper Sadsbury Forge

West Branch, Octorara Creek:
Black Rock Forge, White Rock Forge

Pequea Creek:
Martic Forge

Conestoga River:
Lower Windsor Forge, Pool Forge, Spring Grove Forge, Upper Windsor Forge

Colerain-Little Britain Township:
Black Rock Furnace

Derry Township, now Lebanon County:
Colebrook Furnace

East Drumore Township:
Conowingo Furnace

Eden Township:
Mount Eden Furnace

Elizabeth Township:
Elizabeth Furnace

Lebanon Township, now Lebanon County:
Cornwall Furnace

Martic Township, now Providence Township:
Martic Furnace

Mount Joy Township:
Mount Vernon Furnace

Rapho-Penn townships:
Mount Hope Furnace

Bibliography

Brener, David, *Lancaster's Gates of Heaven, Portals to the Past,* Lancaster: Temple Shaarai Shomayim, 1976.

Ellis, Franklin, and Samuel Evans. *History of Lancaster County, Pennsylvania.* Philadelphia: Everts & Peck, 1883.

Hensel, W. Uhler. *Resources and Industries of Lancaster City.* Lancaster: The Board of Trade, 1887.

Higginbotham, Sanford W. *The Keystone in the Democratic Arch, Pennsylvania Politics, 1800–1816.* Harrisburg: Pennsylvania Historical and Museum Commission, 1952.

Kilburn, Francis. *A Brief History of the City of Lancaster...including the Business Cards of the Principal Merchants and Manufacturers.* Lancaster: Pearsol & Geist, 1870.

Klein, Frederic Shriver. *Lancaster County Since 1841.* Lancaster: The Lancaster County National Bank, 1955.

Klein, Philip Shriver. *Pennsylvania Politics, 1817–1832; A Game Without Rules.* Philadelphia: Historical Society of Pennsylvania, 1940.

———. "Early Lancaster County Politics," *Pennsylvania History III* (April 1936): 98-114.

———. *President James Buchanan.* University Park: The Pennsylvania State University Press, 1962.

Lancaster Planning Commission. *Neighborhood Analysis.* Lancaster: City of Lancaster Planning Commission, 1966.

Lancaster Redevelopment Authority. *Annual Report for 1958.* Lancaster: City of Lancaster Redevelopment Authority, 1958.

Lemon, James T. *The Best Poor Man's Country: A Geographical Study of Early Southeastern Pennsylvania.* Baltimore: The Johns Hopkins Press, 1972.

Loose, John Ward Willson. *The Military Market Basket.* Lancaster: Lancaster County Bicentennial Committee, Inc., 1976.

Nolan, John. *Lancaster, Pennsylvania: A Comprehensive City Plan.* Lancaster: The Lancaster Chamber of Commerce and City of Lancaster Planning Commission, 1929.

Reilly, Richard M. *Resources and Industries of Lancaster, Pennsylvania.* Lancaster: Board of Trade, 1909.

Reninger, Marion Wallace. *Famous Women of Lancaster.* Lancaster: Forry and Hacker, 1965.

———. *Via Mulberry Street and Lime.* Lancaster: Rudisill and Co., 1960.

———. *Orange Street.* Lancaster: Rudisill and Co., 1958.

Riddle, William. *The Story of Lancaster, Pennsylvania, Old and New.* Lancaster: The New Era Printing Co., 1917

Sanderson, Alfred. *History of the Union Fire Company No. 1, 1760-1879.* Lancaster: Inquirer Publishing Co., 1879.

Sullivan, William A. *The Industrial Worker in Pennsylvania, 1800–1840.* Harrisburg: Pennsylvania Historical and Museum Commission, 1955.

Twombley, Clifford Gray. *Report on Vice Conditions in the City of Lancaster.* Lancaster: Law and Order Society of Lancaster, 1915.

Welchans, George R. *History of Lodge No. 43, F. & A.M. of Lancaster, 1785-1935.* Lancaster Lodge No. 43 of Lancaster, 1936.

Wood, Jerome Herman, Jr. *Conestoga Crossroads: The Rise of Lancaster, Pennsylvania, 1730-1789.* Ph.D. dissertation, Brown University, 1969.

Worner, William Frederick. *Old Lancaster Tales and Traditions.* Lancaster: n.p., 1927.

Articles of special interest from the *Journal of the Lancaster County Historical Society*

Barnes, Horace R. "History of the Gas and Electric Industries in Lancaster County." *JLCHS* 52 (1948): 101.

Bowman, John J. "Lancaster's Part in the Watchmaking Industry." *JLCHS* 49 (1945): 29.

Daum, Fred J. "The Cork Industry as Lancaster Knows It." *JLCHS* 54 (1950): 117.

Harbold, Peter Monroe. "Schools and Education in Lancaster Borough." *JLCHS* 46 (1942): 1.

Heiges, George L. "When Lancaster was Capital of Pennsylvania." *JLCHS* 55 (1951): 1; 56 (1952): 45; 57 (1953): 81; 58 (1954): 1.

———. "Lancaster General Hospital: First Twenty Five Years, 1893-1918." *JLCHS* 62 (1958): 174.

Heisey, Martin Luther. "The Borough Fathers." *JLCHS* 46 (1942): 45.

———. "How Lancaster Grew and What People Thought of It." *JLCHS* 45 (1941): 87.

———. "Religious Life in Lancaster Borough." JLCHS 45 (1941): 126.

Kieffer, Elizabeth Clark. "Social Life in Lancaster Borough." *JLCHS* 45 (1941): 105.

———. "Libraries in Lancaster." *JLCHS* 48 (1944): 71.

Klein, Frederic Shriver. "Robert Coleman, Millionaire Ironmaster." *JLCHS* 64 (1960):17.

Teeters, Negley. "Public Executions in Pennsylvania, 1682-1834." *JLCHS* 64 (1960): 85.

Villee, Claude. "A Short History of the Lancaster Fire Department, 1882-1958." *JLCHS* 63 (1959): 137.

LANCASTER COUNTY
The Red Rose of Pennsylvania

By John Ward Willson Loose

"Partners in Progress" by Gary G. Martin and Donald L. Collins

Photographs in opening pages of book by David Hollinger. All photographs courtesy of the Lancaster County Historical Society, unless otherwise specified.

Managing Editor: Linda J. Hreno. *Senior Editor*: Nancy Jackson. *Profiles Editors:* Michael P. Macuk, Jeffrey Reeves. *Design and Art Production*: Elisa Morrison. *Photo Editor:* Robin L. Sterling. *Coordinator:* Kelly Goulding

Published in cooperation with the Lancaster County Historical Society and the Lancaster Chamber of Commerce and Industry by CCA Publications, Inc., 7355 Topanga Canyon Boulevard, Suite 202, Canoga Park, California 91303, 818-710-1627. Nellie C. Scott, *President.*

Library of Congress Cataloging-in-Publication Data

Loose, John Ward Willson.
Lancaster County : the red rose of Pennsylvania / John Ward Willson Loose ; "Partners in Progress" by Gary G. Martin and Donald L. Collins.
p. cm.
Includes bibliographical references and index.
ISBN 1-884166-03-2 : $27.95
1. Lancaster County (Pa.)—History. 2. Lancaster County (Pa.)—Description and travel. 3. Lancaster County (Pa.)—Industries.
I. Title.
F157.L2L75 1994 94-6229
974.8'15—dc20 CIP